Amazing Questions and Answers

This is a Parragon Publishing Book
This edition published in 2004

Parragon Publishing
Queen Street House
4 Queen Street
Bath BA1 1HE, UK

Copyright © Parragon 2001

Original book produced by
David West Children's Books
This edition by
Design Principals, Warminster

British Library Cataloguing-in-Publication Data

A catalogue record for this book is available
from the British Library.

ISBN 1-40540-738-7

Printed in Indonesia

Illustrators
James Field Sarah Lees Terry Riley
Ross Watton (SGA) Rob Shone

Cartoonist
Peter Wilks (SGA)

Editor
James Pickering

Consultant
Steve Parker

Amazing
Questions
and
Answers

Written by
Anita Ganeri, Adam Hibbert, John Malam, Clare Oliver,
Chris Oxlade, James Pickering and Denny Robson

p

CONTENTS

CHAPTER ONE
RACING MACHINES

8 Who raced a horse and carriage in a train?

9 Who first raced in cars?

10 Who used a rocket to go faster than 600 mph?

10 Who put a rocket on a bike?

11 Who went faster than the speed of sound in a car?

12 Which cars race to a formula?

13 What's an Indycar?

13 Which cars race for 24 hours?

14 Who waves a checkered flag?

14 Who wears fireproof underwear?

15 Who works in the pit?

16 Who uses their knees to go round corners?

16 Which motorbike racers have three wheels?

17 Which motorbikes don't have brakes?

18 Who raced hotrods along the street?

19 What were café racers?

19 Who wears a yellow shirt if he's winning?

20 Where do you come first if you are last?

21 Which race cars have no engines?

21 Are there races for trucks?

22 Which record breaker had three hulls?

22 Who races on a cat?

23 Which boats skate on ice?

24 What were Gee Bees?

24 What was the longest air race?

25 When was the first air race?

Who raced a horse and carriage in a train?

In 1825, George Stephenson raced his engine Locomotion against a team of horses, and won. For the first time ever, he showed that a mechanical vehicle could travel more quickly than a horse-drawn carriage.

Locomotion

Amazing! Racing machines have been around for a very long time. The Romans used to race horse-drawn chariots more than 2000 years ago. Their chariots had two wheels which were connected by a wooden axle. It must have been a bumpy ride. The drivers used to stand up to drive, for balance. The more horses, the faster the chariot went.

Is it true?
In 1897, a cyclist beat a motorbike in a race.

Yes. A man called W.J. Stocks pedaled over 27 miles on his bicycle in one hour, and beat a motorbike by 300 yds. The rider of the motorbike was not happy. He said that the crowd was too noisy and had put him off!

Early motor race, France 1902

Who first raced in cars?

The first ever race was in 1894 between Paris and Rouen in France. The Count de Dion won in a steam-powered car, which could only manage 11 mph. Early motor races showed people that cars were as fast and reliable as horses.

Who used a rocket to go faster than 600 mph?

In 1970, American Gary Gabelich drove his rocket-powered car, The Blue Flame, at 631 mph through the Bonneville Salt Flats, and it's still the world's fastest rocket car. When he wasn't breaking records, Gary also raced dragsters and worked as a test astronaut.

Rocket-powered car

Who put a rocket on a bike?
Richard 'Rocketman' Brown started building The Challenger in 1996. It has three rocket engines, which produce about 12,200 horsepower per ton, taking it to 332 mph!

Challenger

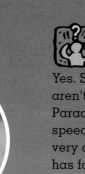

Is it true?
Some cars need parachutes.

Yes. Some cars are so fast that brakes alone aren't powerful enough to stop them. Parachutes drag these cars back to lower speeds when they're traveling very quickly. Thrust SSC has four parachutes to bring it back below the sound barrier.

Who went faster than the speed of sound in a car?

Briton Andy Green set a world record in 1997, when he drove the jet-powered Thrust SSC at 763.035 mph through the Nevada desert.

Thrust SSC

Amazing! As early as 1904, some cars could travel at more than 100 mph! Louis Rigolly was the first person to reach this speed in his enormous 100 horsepower Gobron-Brillié car, during the July Speed Trials in Ostend, Belgium. Luckily he didn't crash. Seatbelts hadn't been invented, and Rigolly only wore a cloth cap to protect his head!

Gobron-Brillié

 Which cars race to a formula?
There are very strict formulas or rules about how race cars are built. Formula One cars' size, shape and gas tank are all governed by rules, so that every race is fair.

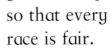 **Amazing!**
Although go-karts are much smaller than other race cars, they can reach speeds of up to 150 mph! Karting is very popular among young drivers, and many Formula One stars, like Michael Schumacher, used to race karts.

FedEx

FedEx

Is it true?
Modern race cars have wings.

Yes. They are at the front and back of the car. A race car's wings are carefully designed to stop the car from taking off. As air passes over the wing, it pulls the car down on to the track. This gives the driver better control and roadholding.

Indycar

What's an Indycar?
Indycar racing takes place at the Indianapolis Motor Speedway in America. They have powerful engines and huge fins.

Ferrari formula one race cars

Le Mans sport car

Which cars race for 24 hours?
Sport cars race around the Le Mans circuit in France for 24 hours. Two or three drivers take turns at the wheel to drive the car as far as possible.

Who waves a checkered flag?

Race officials aren't allowed to talk with drivers during a race, so they communicate with flags. Different flags warn of danger, problems, or may order a driver off the track. The checkered flag is waved in front of the winning car.

| End of race | Danger | Mechanical problems | All clear | The race has been stopped |

Who wears fireproof underwear?

Underneath their overalls, racing drivers must wear fire-resistant 'Nomex' underwear, made up of a long sleeved vest, full length pants, socks and a balaclava. These protect the driver against a blaze of 1480° for twelve seconds.

Amazing! In dry conditions, bald tires provide better grip than tires with grooves. In the rain, cars switch to tires with deep slots, to disperse as much water as possible and prevent skids. Each tire can disperse 6 gallons of water from the road per second!

Is it true?
Race cars could race across the ceiling.

Yes. The air pressure pushing a speeding race car on to the track is so great that they could race upside down.

| Unsportsman-like behavior | Slippery track | Designated car must stop at pits | A driver wants to overtake | Slow vehicle on track |

Who works in the pit?
About 20 mechanics work in the pits, where they make quick repairs and adjustments during a race. They can change a wheel in under five seconds!

Pit crew

Who uses their knees to go round corners?

Riders in motorbike Grands Prix take corners very quickly by leaning sharply into bends, scraping their knee against the track. This is called the 'knee down' position. For protection, they have tough nylon knee pads sewn into their leathers.

Sidecar racing bikes

 Which motorbike racers have three wheels?

Sidecar racing bikes have three wheels. The sidecar isn't powered, but the second rider provides vital balance. On corners, the sidecar rider leans out, for extra roadholding, and the driver hardly has to reduce speed.

Amazing! Some bikes have tires with metal spikes sticking from them, for riding on ice. The spikes pierce the icy surface and stop the bike from skidding. Without them, both bike and rider would go flying!

 Which motorbikes don't have brakes? Speedway racing bikes don't have brakes. Instead, the bike slows to an almost instant halt, as soon as the throttle is released. Riders wear extra sturdy steel boots, which they grind into the dirt, to bring the bike to a final standstill.

Knee down position

Speedway racing bikes

Is it true? Motorbike races last only one hour.

No. Different races have different lengths. The famous Le Mans race in France, for example, lasts for an exhausting 24 hours, while speedway races are often run over just four laps (1300 yards) and last for about a minute!

Who raced hotrods along the street?

There used to be a dangerous trend in America for racing at night through the streets in souped-up road cars, nicknamed 'hotrods'. The official sport of hotrod racing was founded to put an end to racing on the road.

Hotrods

Monte Carlo Grand Prix

Is it true?

Race cars are not allowed to race in cities any more.

No. Several Grands Prix are still run on public highways. The event at Monte Carlo has been held on almost exactly the same circuit since 1929. The Australian Grand Prix in Melbourne is another example. The streets are cleared of public traffic in advance and crash barriers are set up. Dozens of classic car rallies also run from town to town.

What were café racers?

Café racers were specially modified bikes, which were raced to and from roadside cafés. This craze started in England in the 1960s. Not surprisingly, café racing on public highways is against the law!

Amazing! In July 1924, Ernest Eldridge broke the World Land Speed Record on a French public highway. He was driving a specially built 1907 Fiat called Mephistopheles and reached 146 mph!

Mephistopheles

Who wears a yellow shirt if he's winning?

The overall leader in the exhausting Tour de France bicycle race wears a bright yellow shirt. Recently some stages of the race have been run in southern England, Spain and Belgium, as well as France.

Where do you come first if you are last?

A demolition derby is not so much a race as a test of strength. Modified road cars deliberately smash into one another, and the winner is the last car to keep moving. It's a dangerous sport, and drivers are protected by harnesses and safety cages.

Amazing! Some tractors are powered by aircraft engines! Tractor Tuggers have to drag a sledge weighing a hefty 100 tons, for 100 yards along a dirt track.

Tractor Tugger

Gravity Formula One

Which race cars have no engines?

Gravity Formula One cars are downhill racers, which have no engines, just a steering lever and a small brake. Drivers skid them down steep mountain roads at speeds of around 60 mph!

Is it true?
People race lawn mowers.

Yes. Some people really do take their lawn mowers racing. It's cheaper than Formula One, and it keeps the grass down as well. It just goes to show that if it's got wheels, someone out there will race it!

Demolition derby

Are there races for trucks?

Yes. Specially tuned trucks compete on racetracks. They look like ordinary trucks on the road, but they're a lot faster. Some even have jet engines, reaching speeds of over 350 mph!

Racing trucks

Which record breaker had three hulls?

The three-hulled Yellow Pages Endeavour broke the sail-powered water speed record. With an aerofoil sail perched on its tiny hulls, Endeavour had a speed of 46.53 knots and a crew of just two who traveled in a closed cockpit.

Who races on a cat?

Catamarans, or 'cats' for short, are twin-hulled boats which can be raced, sailed for pleasure, or used as passenger boats. They travel through the water more easily than single-hulled boats, and are steadier in rough seas.

Sand yachts

Amazing! Some boats race all the way around the world, using only wind power. The Round The World Yacht Race is held every four years. Highly skilled sailors can even race 'the wrong way' around the world, against the wind and currents.

Is it true? People race yachts on land.

Yes. Three-wheeled sand yachts race along beaches at about 75 mph. Other yachts race along disused railroads, and even across snow!

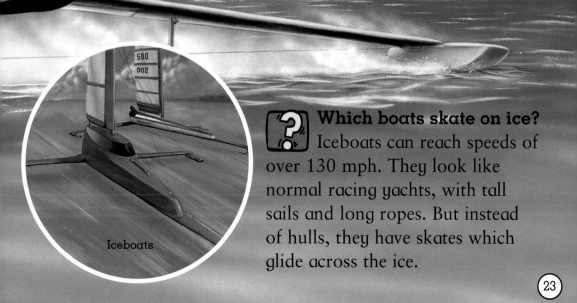

Iceboats

Which boats skate on ice? Iceboats can reach speeds of over 130 mph. They look like normal racing yachts, with tall sails and long ropes. But instead of hulls, they have skates which glide across the ice.

What were Gee Bees?

American Gee Bee planes raced during the 1930s. The company which made them was called Granville Brothers (G.B.). These short, fat planes used to race at speeds of nearly 300 mph, in 5500 mile-long races! Plane races were run to show how reliable the aircraft were.

MacRobertson race

What was the longest air race?

The longest air race was the MacRobertson race from Mildenhall, England to Melbourne, Australia in 1934. It was won by the crew of a de Havilland in a time of 70 hours and 54 minutes.

Is it true?
The first non-stop flight around the world was made in 1933.

No. Wiley Post did make the first solo round the world flight in Winnie Mae in 1933, but he had to stop several times to refuel. It was a 15,596 mile journey, and it took him just over a week.

Winnie Mae

Gee Bees

 Amazing! The first non-stop around the world flight wasn't until 1986. It took Dick Rutan and Jeana Yeager nine days to make the 25,000 miles journey. Their lightweight airplane Voyager had just 18 gallons of fuel left when it landed at Edwards Airforce Base.

Voyager

 When was the first air race?
The first air race was in 1909, near Reims in France. It took place only six years after the very first flight by the Wright brothers.

CHAPTER TWO
SHIPS AND SUBMARINES

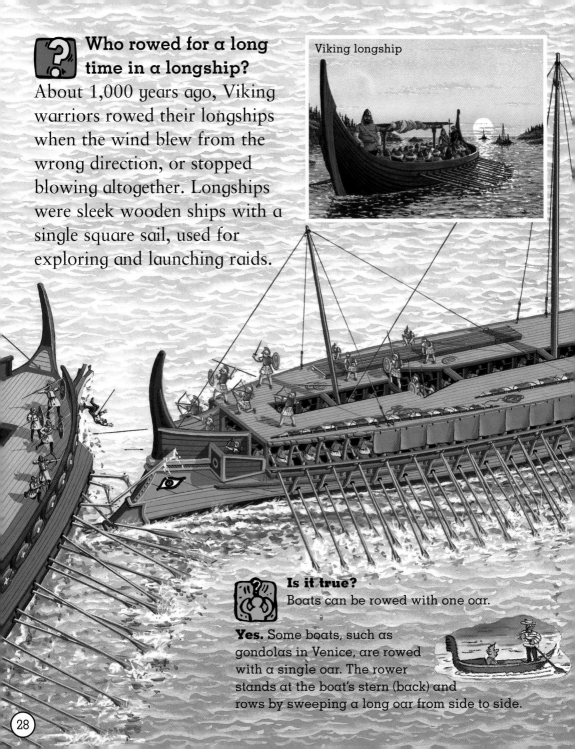

Who rowed for a long time in a longship?

About 1,000 years ago, Viking warriors rowed their longships when the wind blew from the wrong direction, or stopped blowing altogether. Longships were sleek wooden ships with a single square sail, used for exploring and launching raids.

Viking longship

Is it true?
Boats can be rowed with one oar.

Yes. Some boats, such as gondolas in Venice, are rowed with a single oar. The rower stands at the boat's stern (back) and rows by sweeping a long oar from side to side.

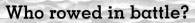

Who rowed in battle?

The Ancient Greeks fought in warships called galleys that they rowed into battle. Slaves did the rowing while soldiers fought on deck. Galleys had a sharp ram at the bow (front) to sink enemy ships. A galley with three banks of oars on each side was called a trireme.

Amazing!
Many people have rowed across the Atlantic Ocean or Pacific Ocean. And some have done it solo (on their own). The journey across the Atlantic takes two months or more, and across the Pacific four months or more.

Ancient Greek trireme

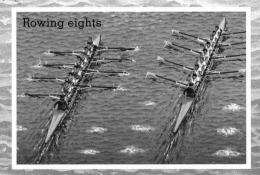

Rowing eights

Who steers an eight?

An 'eight' is the crew of a racing rowing boat. The ninth member, the cox, tells the rowers what pace to row at, and steers with a small rudder at the back of the boat.

Is it true?
Sailors had to climb the masts to change sails.

No. Sailors had to 'go aloft' to change the sails, but they climbed rope ladders instead of the wooden masts themselves. And there were no safety ropes in case of a fall!

What were clippers?

A clipper was a fast-sailing cargo ship. Clippers were built in America and Europe in the 19th century to carry important cargoes, such as tea from China, quickly around the world. Clippers had three or four tall masts with five or more huge sails on each mast.

Clippers

Amazing! Large sailing ships often had a carving called a figurehead at the bow. Some figureheads were gods or saints, some were mythical sea creatures such as mermaids, and some were real people. Viking longships had frightening dragon or snake figureheads.

Mayflower

 ## What was a galleon?

Galleons were trading and fighting ships used in the 15th and 16th centuries. The galleon Mayflower took the first pilgrims to America in 1620.

Who went to sea on a junk?

Chinese sailors have been going to sea in ships called junks for more than a thousand years. Junks have cloth sails strengthened with bamboo poles. Large junks have five masts. Junks were the first ships to have a rudder to help them steer.

Chinese junk

What was a steam liner?

A steam liner was a steam-powered passenger or cargo ship that crossed oceans on set routes at set times. In the 19th and 20th centuries, millions of people emigrated from Europe to America on steam liners, taking their own food and bedding.

Is it true?
Anchors are used to slow ships down.

No. Anchors stop ships from floating away with the wind or tide. Anchors catch in rocks or sand on the seabed.

Amazing! Modern cruise liners are like huge floating hotels. There are cabins for thousands of passengers, restaurants, cinemas, theaters and lots of swimming pools.

Club Med 1

Which modern liner has sails?

The luxury cruise liner Club Med has sails as well as an engine. Using the sails when the wind blows saves fuel for the engine.

RMS Queen Mary (launched 1934)

Tug

What does a tug do?

A tug is a boat with very powerful
engines that pulls or pushes large ships. Tugs
help to move ships in and out of port. They
also go to the rescue of broken-down ships,
and tow them back to port to be repaired.

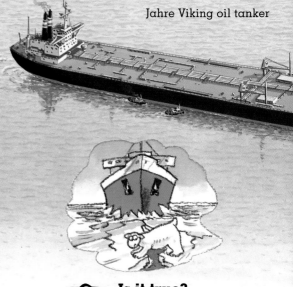
Jahre Viking oil tanker

 ## What is the biggest ship?

The oil tanker Jahre Viking is the biggest ship ever built. It is 1,504 feet long and 226 feet wide. Four soccer pitches would fit on its deck. Fully laden, it weighs 564,000 tons.

 ## What is a ro-ro?

A ro-ro is a type of vehicle ferry. Ro-ro is short for roll-on, roll-off. It means that vehicles such as cars, buses and trucks drive on to the ferry at one port and drive off again when the ferry arrives at its destination.

Is it true?
Some ships break ice.

Yes. Ice breakers are ships that can break through thick ice. They help to keep routes open for other ships in the winter. An ice breaker has powerful engines and a very strong hull.

Ro-ro container ship

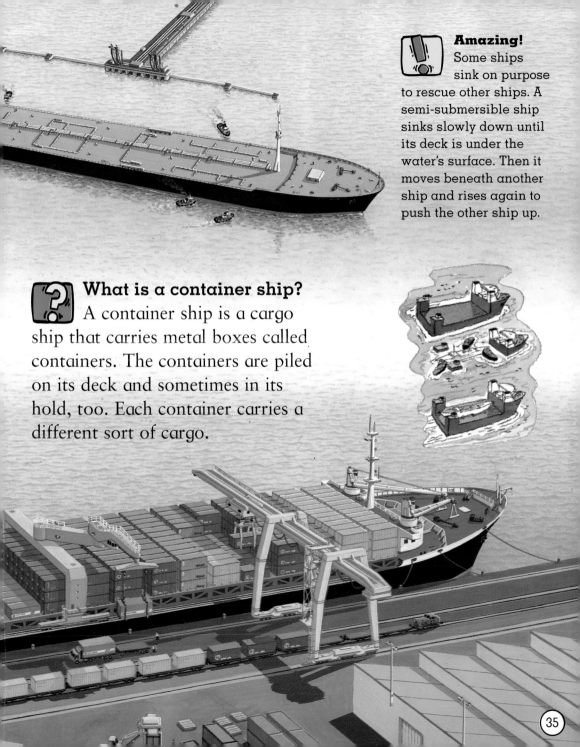

Some ships sink on purpose to rescue other ships. A semi-submersible ship sinks slowly down until its deck is under the water's surface. Then it moves beneath another ship and rises again to push the other ship up.

What is a container ship?

A container ship is a cargo ship that carries metal boxes called containers. The containers are piled on its deck and sometimes in its hold, too. Each container carries a different sort of cargo.

Who trawls the oceans?

Fishermen use boats called trawlers to catch fish and other sea creatures such as shrimp. A trawler moves slowly through the water, pulling huge fishing nets behind. Every few hours the nets are pulled in and emptied. Trawlers have to be very strong and seaworthy because they often fish in stormy seas.

Shrimp trawler

What is a factory ship?

A factory ship is a huge fishing ship where fish are prepared for market. The catch can even be frozen and stored on board. Factory ships sometimes catch their own fish, but normally they store fish caught by a whole fleet of much smaller fishing boats.

Factory ship

Whaling ship

Who hunted whales?

Whalers were men who hunted whales for the oil in their blubber and also for their meat. When a whale was spotted, the whalers went after it in small boats and threw or fired spears, called harpoons, to kill it.

Is it true?

People go fishing in kayaks.

Yes. Kayak is the proper name for a canoe with a deck on top and a small cockpit where the paddler sits. In the Arctic, Inuit fishermen hunt in kayaks made from wooden frames covered in seal skin.

Amazing! Fishing boats called long liners catch fish on a fishing line up to 30 miles long. Hooks with bait are attached all the way along the line. Floats on the line have beacons that show where the line is in the dark.

Which boats are unsinkable?

Lifeboats are rescue boats that don't sink even if they capsize (turn upside down). A lifeboat has a watertight cabin that makes it bob back upright. It has a strong hull and powerful engines for traveling quickly through rough seas.

Lifeboat

Amazing! The famous passenger liner Titanic was supposed to be unsinkable. But it sank on its maiden (first) voyage after hitting an iceberg in the North Atlantic Ocean in 1912.

Lightship

SEVENSTONES

What is a lightship?

A lightship is a ship with a lighthouse on its deck. Lightships are anchored near shallow water or dangerous rocks to warn sailors to keep clear. Most lightships have no crew because they are controlled automatically from shore.

Is it true?
Life savers row through surf to rescue people.

Yes. Lifeguards row boats designed to break easily through surf near the beach. When they're off duty, lifeguards also race their boats.

Fire-fighting tug

Which boat puts out fires?

Fire-fighting tugs are like fire trucks at sea. They're designed to put out fires on ships, oil rigs, or in buildings on shore. They have powerful pumps which pump water from the sea to spray at fires.

Which ship is a floating airfield?

An aircraft carrier has a huge, empty flat deck where aircraft take off and land. The aircraft take off from the bow using a catapult. They land again from the stern. Hooks on the planes catch a wire on deck, and stop the planes with a jolt. Underneath the deck are hangars where the aircraft are stored and serviced.

 Amazing! The first gun battle between two ironclads (warships with iron armor) took place in 1862 during the American Civil War. The Monitor and the Merrimack fired at each other but no great damage was done.

American aircraft carrier

What was a pocket battleship?

Pocket battleships were small, fast, German ships in the 1930s. Only three of them were built. Each had six huge guns, armor more than 2 inches thick and powerful diesel engines.

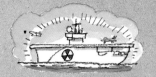

Admiral Graf Spee pocket battleship

Which ship is invisible?

The United States Navy 'stealth' warship doesn't show up clearly on enemy radar. Like the stealth aircraft, its special shape and paint scatter enemy radar signals making it very difficult to detect.

Stealth warship

How big are submarines?

The biggest submarines are nuclear-powered naval submarines. The biggest of all are Russian Typhoon submarines. They're 558 feet long (as long as two soccer pitches) and weigh 26,500 tons. They can stay under water for months on end and sail around the world without refuelling.

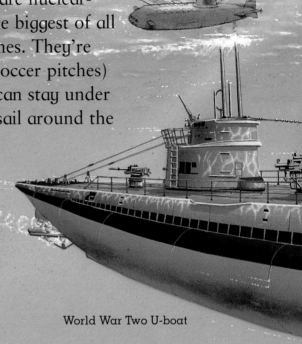

World War Two U-boat

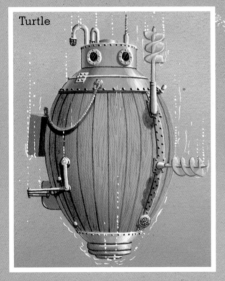

Turtle

Amazing! The first working submarine looked like a wooden barrel. It was built in 1776 and was called Turtle. The operator sat inside and pedaled to make its propellers turn. Turtle was designed to attack ships by diving under them and fixing a bomb to their hulls. But it was never successful.

What was a U-boat?

U-boats were German submarines used in World War One and World War Two. U-boat is short for underwater boat. U-boats sank thousands of ships. They crept up silently, hidden under the water, and fired missiles called torpedoes. The torpedoes zoomed through the water and exploded when they hit the ships.

Is it true?
Submarines use sound to see.

Yes. A submarine's sonar machine makes beeps of sound that spread out through the water. If the sound hits an object in the water, it bounces back to the submarine and is picked up by the sonar machine. The machine works out how big the object is and how far away it is.

Operating the periscope

What is a periscope?
Submarine crews use their periscopes to see ships on the surface above them when submarines are submerged. The top of the periscope sticks just above the surface. It works using several lenses and prisms (triangular pieces of glass).

? What is a micro-sub?

A micro-sub (also called a submersible) is a small submarine, often used for exploring under the sea. One of the latest micro-subs is Deep Flight 1, which can dive to a depth of 3,280 feet.

Micro sub

Amazing!

Divers who repair undersea pipelines and oil rigs wear strong diving suits, like mini submersibles. They can dive to about 1,000 feet. The divers have to breathe oxygen mixed with helium, which gives them very squeaky voices!

? Is it true?

Submarines can dive to the bottom of the ocean.

No. The deepest a normal submarine can dive is about 2,300 feet. If a submarine went any deeper the huge water pressure would crush its hull and water would flood in.

Jason Junior

Alvin

What are Alvin and Jason Junior?

Alvin is a submersible that carries a crew of three. Jason Junior is a robot submersible that can be operated from Alvin or from a ship on the surface. In 1985, Jason Junior discovered the wreck of the ocean liner Titanic at the bottom of the Atlantic Ocean.

How deep can submersibles go?

Special, extra-strong-hulled submersibles called bathyscaphes can dive many miles under the sea. In 1960, the bathyscaphe Trieste made the deepest dive ever – an incredible 35,800 feet into the Marianas Trench in the Pacific Ocean.

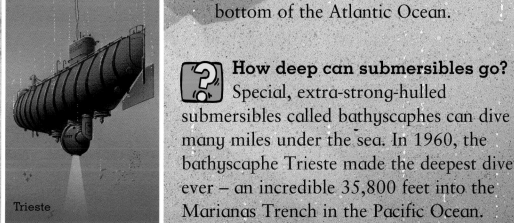

Trieste

CHAPTER THREE
CARS

What was a horseless carriage?

A horseless carriage was a horse-drawn carriage with an engine in place of the horse. The first horseless carriages were powered by steam. In England by the 1830s some passenger services were operated with steam coaches. But the coaches were slow, noisy and dirty, and wrecked the cart tracks!

Daimler and his first car

Who invented the first car?

Two German engineers, Karl Benz and Gottlieb Daimler, both built working cars in 1885. Each car had a small gas engine to drive it.

James's steam carriage 1829

Amazing! When mechanical vehicles first appeared in Britain, a man had to walk in front of them carrying a red warning flag (or a red light at night). The Red Flag Law was introduced because other road users, such as horse riders, complained about the danger.

Is it true?
The first cars didn't have steering wheels.

Yes. The steering wheel did not appear on cars until the late 1890s. Before that, drivers steered with a lever, like the tiller on a boat, or by spinning handles on a small upright wheel on the end of a vertical pole.

Which was the first car to be sold?

The first car to be sold was a three-wheel model built by Karl Benz. The first owner was a French engineer called Emile Roger, who bought his car in 1887. Soon Benz had a factory building cars for sale, but only a few of the three-wheelers were sold.

Benz Patent-Motorwagen

Who got dressed up to go motoring?

Drivers and passengers of early cars had to dress up in protective clothes before driving into the countryside. Most cars had no windshield, doors or bodywork to keep out wind and rain, or dust and mud from the dirt roads. So people wore thick fur coats or rubber capes, peaked hats and enormous goggles over their eyes.

 Amazing! In the early 1900s, there were no gas stations. Village blacksmiths often kept a supply of gas to sell to car drivers whose tanks had run dry. There were no garages or mechanics either, so drivers had to carry a tool kit and spare parts in their cars, in case of a breakdown.

What was a 'Tin Lizzie'?

The Model-T Ford was nicknamed 'Tin Lizzie'. It was small and reliable, and cheap enough for millions of people to buy.

Model-T Ford

Is it true?

Henry Ford invented the production line.

No. Production lines existed before Henry Ford started making cars. But he did invent the moving line, where the cars moved along as parts were added.

Who spoke to the driver through a tube?

In some early cars, the passengers sat in the back behind a glass screen. The driver sat in the front. The passengers spoke to the driver through a metal tube to give him directions.

Austin Landaulet 1911

Who drove a Silver Ghost?

The Silver Ghost was one of the first cars built by the Rolls Royce company. Only rich people could afford to buy one, and they normally employed a chauffeur to drive it! Like all Rolls Royce cars, the Silver Ghost was famous for being very quiet and extremely well made.

Austin 7

Which car was very cheap to run?

The Austin Seven was so economical that it used just under a cent's worth of gas to travel a mile. The Seven was so tiny that it was often called a 'toy' car, but it was very cheap to buy.

Is it true?
Taxis have always had meters.

Yes. The word taxi is short for taximeter cab. A taximeter was a meter designed in 1891 that recorded the distance that a horse-drawn cab had traveled. When engine-powered taxis were introduced in 1907, they also had to have a meter.

Who went on trips in a charabanc?

Factory workers and their families used to go on days out to the seaside or to the city in a vehicle called a charabanc. A charabanc was like a wagon with benches in the back for passengers to sit on. The first charabancs were pulled by teams of horses.

Rolls Royce Silver Ghost

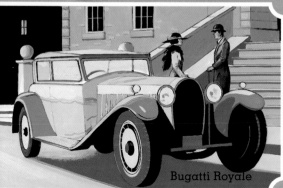

Bugatti Royale

Amazing! The Bugatti Type 41 Royale was designed by Ettore Bugatti to be the most luxurious car ever. His idea was that every royal family in Europe would buy one. The car was seven yards long, but only six Royales were ever built, and only three were ever sold. Today, if a Bugatti Royale ever appears at auction, it fetches millions of pounds.

What was the 'Tin Goose'?

'Tin Goose' was the nickname of a short-lived rear-engined car called the Tucker '48. It had many original features, such as a strong passenger safety compartment and a third headlight which swivelled as the driver turned the steering wheel.

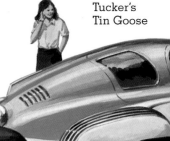

Tucker's Tin Goose

Citroën Traction Avant

Why was the Citroën 7CV so special?

The Citroën 7CV of 1934 was the first popular car driven by its front wheels. It was known as the Traction Avant. It was also one of the first cars to have a one-piece body shell instead of a chassis with a body built on top.

Amazing! Even as late as 1931, some cars ran on steam power. Abner Doble built his first steam car in 1905, and went on to make several luxurious examples. They had plenty of power, and ran almost silently, but at prices between $8,000 and $11,000, they were beyond the reach of the average motorist.

What was the people's car?

The people's car was the first Volkswagen (which means 'people's car' in German). It was designed in the 1930s by Doctor Ferdinand Porsche to be a small family car which was cheap to run. It was soon nicknamed the Beetle or Bug. 40 million have been made.

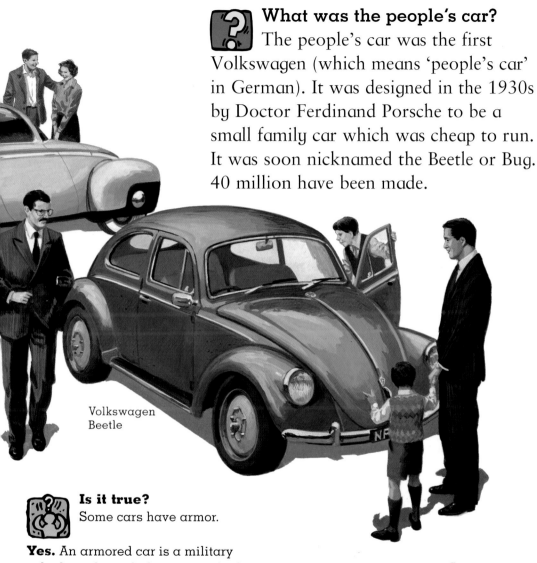

Volkswagen Beetle

Is it true?
Some cars have armor.

Yes. An armored car is a military vehicle with steel plates on its body to make it bullet-proof. It usually has a small gun, too. Security companies often use vans with armor to transport valuable items or cash. Some limousines also have armor plating to make them bullet proof.

Which car could really fly?

In 1949, American inventor Molt Taylor built a car which could be turned into a plane. By 1953, the car had flown over 25,000 miles. On the ground, the Aerocar towed its tail and wings in a trailer.

Aerocar without wings

Is it true?

American cars had the biggest fins of all.

Yes. In the 1950s, American car designers began adding pointy bits such as tail fins to their cars. Some features were copied from the jet fighters of the time! Tail fins often had rows of lights up the back. These huge and thirsty cars also had plenty of chrome bodywork.

Amazing! The driver of a Cadillac Coupe de Ville did not have to worry about blinding other drivers with his or her headlights. The car had an electronic eye which detected headlights coming in the opposite direction and automatically dipped its headlights.

Which car had gull wings?

The doors on the 1952 Mercedes 300SL opened upwards like a gull's wings. The idea was given up because they couldn't be opened if the car turned over in an accident.

Mercedes gull-wing

What was a T-bird?

T-bird was the nickname given to the Ford Thunderbird. The first model appeared in 1953. It was a huge two-seater convertible. In the 1950s, American manufacturers built many huge gas guzzlers like the Thunderbird.

Ford Thunderbird

? What was Willys jeep?

Until the middle of World War Two, Willys-Overland Company made ordinary cars. But they became famous for producing one of the best known cars of all time. The Willys jeep was a four-wheel drive general purpose (G.P.) vehicle, used by the American army.

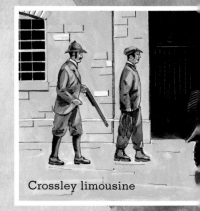
Crossley limousine

Willys jeep

? What is four-wheel drive?

When a car has four-wheel drive, it means that the engine makes all four wheels turn. In most cars, the engine only turns two of the wheels. Four-wheel drive is excellent for traveling off-road on muddy tracks and up steep hills.

Is it true?
A car has been driven on the Moon.

Yes. The missions Apollo 15, 16 and 17 that traveled to the Moon in the 1970s carried Lunar Roving Vehicles (LRVs) or Moon buggies. The astronauts drove the electric buggies around the Moon's surface, looking for interesting rocks. All three buggies are still on the Moon.

Amazing! King George V of England owned a six-wheeled limousine. It was built by Crossley in 1929, and had a 3.8 liter, six cylinder engine. The king used it for cross country expeditions, but it never went into production.

Which car can swim?

The 1962 Amphicar was part car, part boat. It had two propellers at the back, and the front wheels steered it, like a rudder. The large tail fins stopped water from flooding the engine.

Amphicar

How do robots make cars?

Factory robots weld and paint cars on production lines. They are taught what to do by an engineer and then do it again and again very accurately. They work 24 hours a day and never get tired!

Robot production line

Who crash-tests cars?

Crash-test dummies are artificial humans which sit inside cars as they're made to crash. The electronic dummies measure what happens to them, and if the cars' safety features work properly. Cars which fail the tests have to be re-designed.

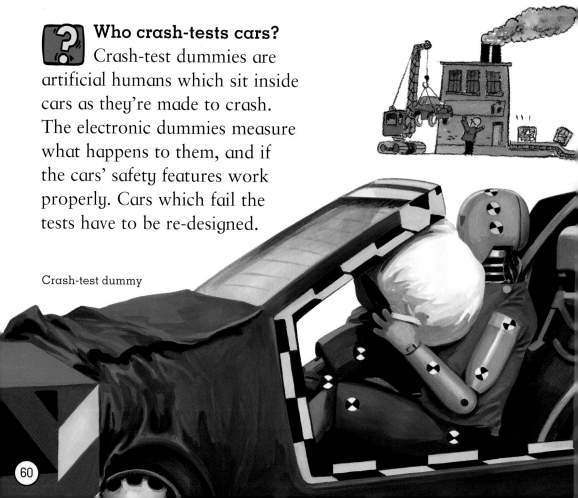
Crash-test dummy

 How are cars designed?
Every part of a car is designed using computers. Engineers draw what the parts and the car will look like, and the computer helps to control the machines which make the parts.

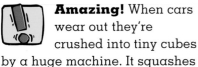

Amazing! When cars wear out they're crushed into tiny cubes by a huge machine. It squashes the car first one way and then the other. The metal in the cube is recycled to make new cars.

 Is it true?
Cars are tested in wind tunnels.

Yes. A wind tunnel is a tube with a huge fan at one end. Engineers check how air flows around the cars. The easier it flows, the faster the car can go and the less fuel it uses.

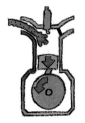

1 Fuel and air are drawn into the cylinder.

2 Fuel-air mixture is squeezed by the piston.

3 The mixture is ignited by a spark which forces the piston down.

4 The piston forces the exhaust gases out

What is an internal combustion engine?

An internal combustion engine is the sort of engine that most cars have. 'Internal combustion' means that a fuel and air mixture burns inside can-shaped cylinders inside the engine.

Engine

Brakes

Suspension

Tire with tread

Why do cars have gears?

Cars have gears so that they can start off and move at different speeds. First gear is for starting off. First and second gears are for going slowly. Fourth and fifth gears are for going quickly.

 Is it true?
The tread of a tire grips the road.

No. The rubber of the tires grips the road. Tread is the pattern of grooves around the outside of a tire. The grooves let water escape from between a tire and a wet road so that the rubber can touch the road surface for grip.

Austin-Healey 3000 Mk III

What are springs and dampers?

Springs and dampers make up a car's suspension, which gives the people inside a smooth ride. Springs let the car's wheels move up and down as it goes over bumps. Dampers stop the car from bouncing after it's passed over the bumps.

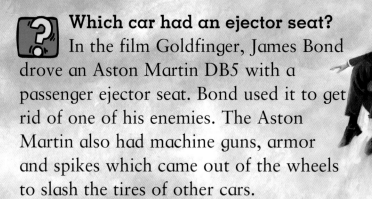

Which car had an ejector seat?

In the film Goldfinger, James Bond drove an Aston Martin DB5 with a passenger ejector seat. Bond used it to get rid of one of his enemies. The Aston Martin also had machine guns, armor and spikes which came out of the wheels to slash the tires of other cars.

Aston Martin DB5

BMT 214A

Amazing! When the Pope travels away from the Vatican, he takes a special car, nicknamed the 'Popemobile'. The car has a bullet-proof glass dome. When the Pope goes on tours he stands under the dome holding on to a hand rail. His followers can easily see him, and he can see them, without the risk of attack.

John Lennon's Rolls Royce

 Who had his Rolls Royce painted in amazing flowery patterns?

The Beatles were the world's biggest pop group in the 1960s. Singer John Lennon painted his Rolls Royce Phantom VI with trendy colorful patterns.

 Is it true?
There really was a car called a Chitty Chitty Bang Bang.

Yes. In the 1920s, Count Louis Zborowski commissioned three incredibly fast Brooklands race cars. The Count, a keen racer, competed in all three cars, but was killed in his Mercedes race car in 1924.

 Which supercar had six wheels?

The wedge-shaped Panther Six was designed by Bob Jankel in 1977. It was sixteen feet long, and over six feet wide. Both pairs of front wheels steered the car, which was never sold to the public.

Panther Six

Which car can shorten itself?

The Renault Zoom is a tiny car which can get shorter by folding its rear wheels up. This makes it easier to park in smaller parking spaces. The Zoom also has a 'green' electric motor, which is powered by rechargeable batteries.

WEST ROAD

Zoom cars

Which is the cleanest car?

The NECAR 4 is powered by liquid hydrogen, which is stored in a cylinder at the back of the car. The fuel is passed through a fuel cell, which creates the electricity to power the car. These cars are quiet and efficient, and instead of dirty exhaust fumes, they only produce water.

Is it true?
Cars can run on plants.

Yes. In Brazil there's an alternative source of fuel, taken directly from a plant. One "gas tree" is able to produce nearly five gallons of fuel. The Brazilians are planning to grow huge plantations of these trees to solve the problem of increasing fuel shortages.

NECAR 4

ecar 4

 ## Which car runs on sunlight?
Cars are being developed that can convert sunlight into electricity to power their engines. The solar-powered car of the future might look like the vehicle pictured below, with solar panels on the roof.

Prototype
solar car

CHAPTER FOUR
TRAINS

Which train was pulled by horses?

Between 1800 and 1825, there were 'trains' without engines in Wales and Austria. Horses pulled carriages along the rails. It was a smoother ride than road travel.

Which train was the first to carry passengers?

Stephenson's Locomotion was the first engine to be used on a public railroad, the Stockton and Darlington, England, in 1825. Stephenson's Rocket won a large cash prize in a competition four years later.

Locomotion

Trevethick's 'Catch Me Who Can', 1808

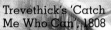

What was the first train engine?

Richard Trevithick, a mine engineer, first demonstrated a mobile engine on rails in 1804. It pulled 70 men and ten tonnes of iron ore, in front of a crowd of amazed onlookers. His next engine became a fairground ride.

Horse-drawn railway

Amazing! There were horse-drawn trains 50 years ago! The Fintona Branch of Ireland's Great Northern railway remained horse-powered until the early 1950s.

Is it true?
The ancient Greeks had a steam engine!

Yes. Hero of Alexander wrote about a steam-powered spinning ball, called the 'aeolipile' in 200 BC. But since slave labor was free, no one bothered to use the engine as a labor-saving device.

Couplings

How do trains fit together?

Trains use special links called couplings to clip different parts together. Trains used to be coupled by hand, which could be dangerous.

What's a locomotive?

A locomotive is the part of the train which contains the engine. It does the work of pulling (or pushing) the train along the track. Locomotives may have to carry their fuel with them. They have special wheels to grip the track.

American Baldwin locomotive

Who steers the train?

Trains follow the track they're on, so they don't need a steering wheel. A person in the junction box can change the direction of a train by moving special junctions in the track called points.

Junction box

Amazing! Some trains lean over! Modern fast trains take corners so quickly that passengers might slosh around inside. Computers in the train 'feel' the sideways forces, and tilt the train in the other direction so that you don't spill your tea.

Is it true?
Some trains are blown along by the wind.

Yes. At least, some were, especially when fuel was hard to find. America's Baltimore & Ohio railroad experimented with sail power in the 1830s.

What diesel was a 'centipede'?

America's Pennsylvania Railroad used Baldwin diesel engines in pairs. Each one had twelve small wheels on each side. Linked together, making a 6,000 horse-power monster, they looked like they had 24 'legs'.

1924 Kitson-Still

Amazing! Diesel engines can be steam engines too. The 1924 Kitson-Still used a diesel engine for its main power, but also used the heat of the engine to create steam. This powered an extra set of drive wheels.

Why did diesel take over from steam?

Diesel power first came into use to cope with the problem of smoke in cities and underground railways. During World War Two, military diesel engines became lighter and smaller. Just like today's trains, the engines fitted under the floors of the carriages.

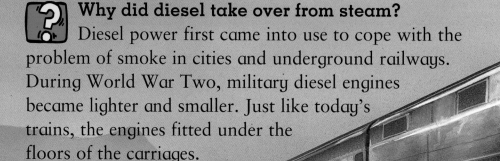

Which diesel looked like a plane?

The German Kruckenburg of 1931 had a huge propeller at the back which pushed it along like a plane on rails. It reached speeds up to 142 mph during a six-mile speed trial. Unfortunately, it was too noisy and dangerous for everyday use.

1931 Kruckenburg

American E Class passenger diesel

Is it true?
Diesel engines use electric motors.

Yes. Many diesel-engined trains actually use electric motors to turn the wheels. The engine itself uses diesel fuel. It turns a generator, which creates the electricity needed by the electric motors. This is because electric motors turn powerfully at all speeds, unlike a diesel engine.

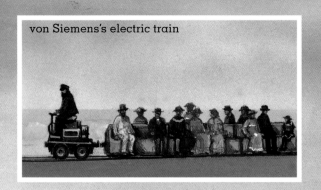
von Siemens's electric train

Is it true?
Electric trains were invented in 1879.

Yes. Werner von Siemens demonstrated an electric train at the Berlin Trades Exhibition, in Germany in 1879. People queued up to have a ride on the tiny carriages.

Which country went electric first?

France was the first country to use electric trains on a major mainline route, making the whole of the Paris to Orléans route electric in 1900. French electric trains have broken many speed records. This 1981 train was able to travel as fast as 326 mph, which was a record at the time.

What's a pantograph?

A pantograph is the metal connecter that reaches from the roof of an electric engine to the live wire overhead – just like the pole at the back of a fairground bumper car.

Amazing! One electric train travels all over Europe. Trans-Europ-Express was designed to use the different electricity supplies in different European countries. Engineers have to change its wheels though, every time it travels in and out of Spain.

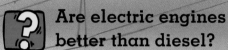

Underground train

Are electric engines better than diesel?

Electric power lets trains use energy without creating too much mess. The only pollution is at the power station where the electricity is made. Electric power is ideal for trams and underground trains in cities. Diesels are better on long routes where great lengths of electricity would be too expensive.

French TGV high-speed train, 1981

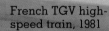

San Francisco cable car

 Which trains travel by cables?
Cable cars, such as the ones in San Francisco, are pulled along by a moving loop of cable, made from strong steel. The cable passes through a slot between the rails, and the cars fix on to it. This way, cable cars can climb very steep hills.

 Where is the longest straight?
It's difficult to build straight stretches of track near towns, but much easier in empty parts of the world. The longest stretch of straight track is in the desert of Australia. It is perfectly straight for 297 miles.

Amazing! Railroads can go missing! During the American Civil War, the South ripped up some of its less important railroads to use as spare parts along the battle front. The states of Florida and Texas gave up their entire networks!

Is it true?
America's rail network is longer than the equator!

Yes. If all the train track in America was laid end-to-end it would form a single track which would go almost six times around the world – that's 150,000 miles!

Can trains travel the length of Africa?

There is no direct link from Cairo in North Africa to Cape Town, South Africa, 6,050 miles away. Cecil Rhodes tried to build a railroad in the late 19th century, but one of his problems was finding enough workmen. Twenty eight of his men were eaten by lions on the Athi Plains in Kenya! However there are plans to complete this link soon.

Australian Indian Pacific railway

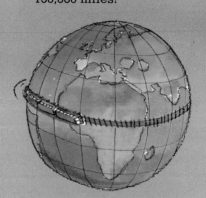

Tunnel-boring machine

 Is the Channel Tunnel longest?

Not quite. The Channel Tunnel is 31 miles in total. The Seikan, Japan's tunnel between the main islands of Honshu and Hokkaido, travels an amazing 33.46 miles underground.

Royal Albert Bridge, spanning the River Tamar, England

How do trains cross rivers?

Trains use big bridges or deep tunnels to cross the largest rivers. The Victorian engineer, Isambard Kingdom Brunel, invented strong metal bridges to carry the weight of a train. Some bridges are so big that repainting them is a full-time job!

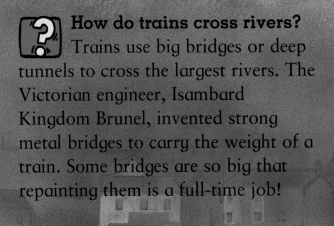

New York Elevated Railway

 Where was the first raised city railroad?

New York City had a serious traffic problem in the 1880s, and that was before cars! An 'Elevated Railroad', known as 'the L' for short, was built above the streets. It still works today.

 Amazing! You can take a train on a boat. Train ferries started operating in the late 1800s between England and France. Passengers stayed in their seats all the way from London to Paris!

 Is it true? Box Hill tunnel knows its creator's birthday.

Yes. Brunel built it at a special angle. Each year, only on his birthday, the sun shines right through the entire two mile tunnel in southern England.

I.K.BRUNEL

What was the biggest train crime?

In 1963 a train full of used banknotes was robbed in Buckinghamshire, England. The thieves got away with over £2.5 million, a huge sum of money even today.

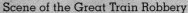

Scene of the Great Train Robbery

Amazing! Trains at Mwatate Dam have to mind out for demons. The Kenyan villagers nearby, thought that trains were having a lot of accidents there because the local spirits were angry. Trains began pausing briefly to salute the spirits, and there hasn't been a crash since!

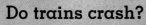 ## Do trains crash?

Trains occasionally crash for a number of reasons – there might be a points failure, or a weak bridge. Amazingly, no one was killed when this cattle train crashed through the front of an Irish railroad station. Rail travel is usually very safe though.

Train crash, Harcourt Street Station, Dublin

? Did railroad projects always work?

No. The English almost built a Channel Tunnel in 1883. They tunneled over a mile under the sea, but the government was worried the French would use the tunnel to invade England, so it was abandoned!

 Is it true?
Some trains are too big.

Yes. The Soviet Union made a locomotive in 1934 that was too long. Its non-swiveling wheels and heavy weight actually straightened out curves in the track, leaving it stuck in a ditch!

Derailment, Russia 1934

How long is the longest train?

The longest train ever was a freight train measuring 4.5 miles! The longest passenger train was a measly 1,895 yards, but the Belgian railway couldn't find a platform long enough to park it!

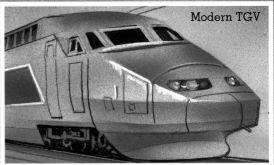

Modern TGV

Track-laying

Amazing! Eight men can lay ten miles of track in a day! A team of eight track-layers in America set this world record on 18 April, 1869.

Which train is fastest?

France pioneered fast trains after World War Two When Japan introduced the Shinkansen 'bullet train' in the 1960s, France responded with the TGV. An experimental TGV has reached 320 mph!

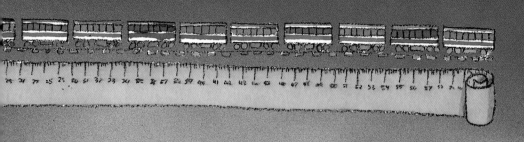

 Is it true?
A train can weigh more than the Eiffel Tower.

Yes. An Australian mine train was weighed in 1996 at 72,191 tons – that's more than eight Eiffel Towers!

Trans-
Siberian
Express

Which train travels farthest?
The once-daily service between Moscow and Vladivostock in Russia travels 5,864 miles, taking eight days. Known as the Trans-Siberian Express, or The Russia, the train has featured in several books and films. It is second only in fame to the Orient Express.

Which train flies?

Really fast future trains might not bother with wheels. They could ride on a cushion of air, like a hovercraft. The nose of the train squashes air underneath its belly as it jets along, and the squashed air lifts it above the ground. The Aerotrain already exists as an experimental vehicle.

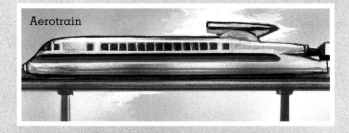
Aerotrain

 Amazing! One sled traveled at Mach 8. An unmanned rocket vehicle on rails achieved 6,121 mph in an American experiment in 1982. On straight track, it could make the eight-day Trans-Siberian trip in less than one hour!

What is a bullet train?

Japan's fastest trains, the Shinkansen, were nicknamed bullet trains because of their pointy noses – and high speed! The fastest, Nozomi, travels at 185 mph. With no time wasted at airports, traveling by Nozomi can be quicker than flying by jet!

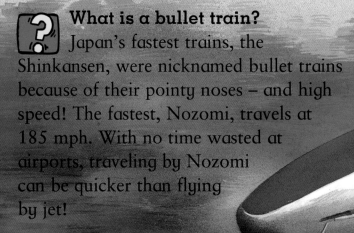

Is it true?
Some trains run on
magnets.

Yes. Germany and Japan have
both tested trains that use
repelling magnets to float above
the track. The track doesn't wear
out, and the trains can slip
along at amazing speeds.

Are trains 'green'?

Trains are less harmful
to the environment than most
other kinds of transport. They
are particularly important in
cities, where underground
trains, trams and monorails
can reduce pollution from cars,
buses and taxis. For long
distance journeys, trains use
much less fuel than jet aircraft.

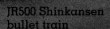

JR500 Shinkansen
bullet train

CHAPTER FIVE
MOTORBIKES

90 Who was the first to put pedals on a bike?

90 What was a penny farthing?

91 What was a safety bicycle?

92 Which bike had a steam engine?

92 Who put an engine above a front wheel?

93 What did the first motorbike look like?

94 What is a drive shaft?

94 What were leather belts for?

95 When was a drive chain first used?

96 Where is a motorbike's engine located?

96 Are motorbike engines all the same shape?

97 What is a two-stroke engine?

98 What is a scooter?

98 Which is the best-selling motorbike ever?

99 Which scooter fits in a car trunk?

100 What is a trials bike?

100 Which bikes have knobbly tires?

101 Which motorcyclists wear armor?

102 What is a TT race?

102 Who raced on wooden boards?

103 What is a superbike?

104 What is a chopper?

105 Who reached 345 kph on a Triumph?

105 Who put three engines on a motorbike?

106 What is stunt riding?

106 What is the wall of death?

107 What is freestyle motocross?

Who was the first to put pedals on a bike?

In 1838, a Scottish blacksmith called Kirkpatrick Macmillan built the first bicycle with pedals. Before this, bicycle riders kicked the ground to move along.

Kirkpatrick Macmillan

Penny farthing

What was a penny farthing?

A penny farthing was a bicycle of the 1870s, named after two British coins. It had an enormous front wheel (the penny) and a small rear wheel (the farthing).

Amazing! In the 1880s, couples often rode side by side on tricycles (cycles with three wheels) called sociables. Each person had a set of pedals, which turned the huge rear wheels.

Is it true?
People raced tricycles.

Yes. In the 1880s, the tricycle was not just a cycle for children, as it is today. It was popular with adults too. Tricycle racing was one of the first forms of cycle racing. Race events were held on bumpy roads and wooden tracks.

What was a safety bicycle?

The safety bicycle was the first bicycle to look like today's bikes. It appeared in 1885. It had two wheels the same size, a diamond-shaped metal frame, pedals that turned the rear wheel using a chain, and brakes worked by levers on the handlebars.

Safety bicycle

Which bike had a steam engine?

The Michaux-Perreaux bicycle of 1869 had a steam engine under its saddle. Wood or coal had to be put in the engine every few minutes to keep the water boiling, to work the engine.

Michaux-Perreaux 1869

Who put an engine above a front wheel?

The Werner brothers in France built a motorbike in 1899. It was a safety bicycle with a gas engine above the front wheel, in front of the handlebars.

Werner 1899

 Amazing!
American engineer Lucius Copeland made a motorbike by adding a small steam engine to a penny farthing. He rode the bicycle backwards, using the small wheel to steer. The machine could travel at 12 mph.

❓ What did the first motorbike look like?

The first proper motorbike had a heavy wooden frame, wooden wheels with metal rims, and two stabilizing wheels to stop it toppling over. It was the first motorbike to have a lightweight gas engine, but it was very slow. It was built by German engineers Daimler and Maybach in 1885.

Daimler/Maybach
1885

Is it true?
Early motorbikes had pedals.

Yes. The engines on early motorbikes were not very powerful or reliable. So the bikes had pedals for going up hills or in case of a breakdown. Some modern bikes, such as mopeds, still have pedals.

93

What is a drive shaft?

A drive shaft is a rod which carries power from a bike's engine to its rear wheel. Some early bikes, such as the Belgian FN of 1906, had drive shafts instead of belts or chains. The shaft turned the wheel using gears.

Amazing! In the early 1900s, women always wore dresses, even when they rode on motorbikes. So some bikes had a dress guard made of string which stopped dresses getting tangled in the engine or rear wheel.

FN 1906

What were leather belts for?

Most motorbikes today use a chain to drive the rear wheel. But many motorbikes made before 1910 used a thick leather belt instead. Belts were unreliable, as they wore out quickly, often broke and even slipped in the rain!

When was a drive chain first used?

Most modern bikes have a flexible metal chain which carries power from the engine to the rear wheel. Chain drives were introduced on some bikes in the early 1900s, such as the 1905 Scott. Chains are made up of dozens of short pieces linked together.

Two-stroke Scott 1905

Douglas 1911

Is it true?

Belt drives are still used today.

Yes. Most modern bikes use a chain drive, but some have belts instead. The belts are made from rubber, strengthened with fabric. Belts are lighter than chains and need less maintenance. A few modern bikes have drive shafts instead of a chain or belt.

Where is a motorbike's engine located?

A motorbike's engine is between the two wheels, attached to the bike's frame. Above the engine, just in front of the driver's seat, is the gas tank. Exhaust pipes carry waste gases from the engine to the rear of the bike.

Fuel tank

Exhaust pipes

Cylinder head

V-Twin engine

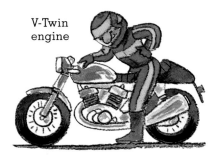

 ## Are motorbike engines all the same shape?

The shape of an engine depends on how many cylinders it has and how they are arranged. A v-twin engine has two cylinders in a V shape. A straight-four has four cylinders in a line.

Yamaha 1600cc

 Amazing! The biggest engine on a motorbike is a 1600 cc engine on a Yamaha superbike. The engine is as big and powerful as the engine in a family car.

Piston

Spark plug ignites fuel-air mixture

Fuel and air explode

Exhaust gases are released

Piston moves down.

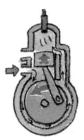

Fuel-air mixture enters cylinder

Piston moves up

Fuel-air mixture is compressed

What is a two-stroke engine?

A two-stroke engine is a simple gas engine often used on small motorbikes, mopeds and scooters. Larger motorbikes have a four-stroke gas engine. Two-stroke engines use more fuel and make more pollution.

What is a scooter?

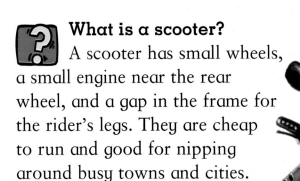

A scooter has small wheels, a small engine near the rear wheel, and a gap in the frame for the rider's legs. They are cheap to run and good for nipping around busy towns and cities.

Amazing!
You can buy toy motorbikes which are models of real bikes, with tiny engines and the same controls as a full-sized bike. They're not allowed on the highway though.

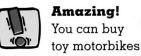
Italjet Millennium 125

Which is the best-selling motorbike ever?

The 50 cc Honda Super Cub, which went on sale in 1958, is the biggest selling motorbike ever. This little bike is cheap to run, and is still popular all over the world.

 Is it true?
The scooter is a
recent invention.

No. Scooters became popular
in Italy in the 1950s, and in
the 1960s they became very
trendy. They were ridden by
young British men called
mods, who dressed in green
parka coats and customized
their scooters with lots of
mirrors and flags.

Yamaha YP 250
Majesty

 **Which scooter fits in a car
trunk?**

The American-made Autoped, which
was produced in 1915, could be folded
up to fit into the trunk of a car. In recent
years, as traffic has become busier, fold-
up scooters have become popular again
for cheap and speedy travel.

21st century scooter

99

Amazing!
Trials bikes can make short hops up almost vertical rock faces. The rider needs good balance and expert control of the clutch and gears.

What is a trials bike?

Trials bikes are designed for riding on steep, rough and rocky ground. They are ridden in motorbike trials, where riders have to ride over obstacles without stopping or putting their feet down to balance.

Which bikes have knobbly tires?

Trials bikes and motocross bikes have tires with a deep, knobbly tread around the outside. The tread helps the tires to grip the wet and muddy ground during competitions.

Motocross

Trials bike

Is it true?
No one has crossed the desert on a motorbike.

No. Riders often take part in motocross competitions held in deserts. There are also long-distance desert motorbike rallies, such as the Paris-Dakar rally which crosses the dusty Sahara Desert.

Paris-Dakar rally

 Which motorcyclists wear armor?
Riders in motocross races wear tough plastic body armor to protect them in case they fall off, or are hit by other bikes. They also wear long, tough boots, helmets and goggles to keep mud out of their eyes.

What is a TT race?

 TT races are held every year on the public highways of the Isle of Man, part of the British Isles. TT stands for Tourist Trophy because, when the races started in 1907, they were for touring motorbikes.

Norton Isle of Man TT racer

1915 Harley-Davidson

Is it true?

All motorbikes have brakes.

No. Motorbikes built for speedway racing have no brakes, and only one gear. These races take place on oval tracks made of dirt, sand, grass, and sometimes ice. The riders slide round the bends at each end of the track.

Who raced on wooden boards?

Early motorbike races used to take place on wooden bicycle tracks. Imagine the splinters if you fell off!

Amazing! In high-speed crashes, motorbike racers sometimes skid across the ground at 150 mph! So racers wear leather overalls to protect them in case they fall off. They also have tough knee pads sewn into their leathers because their knees touch the road as they lean into bends.

What is a superbike?

A superbike, such as this Ducati, is a very fast motorbike, normally with an engine of 750 cc or bigger. The word 'superbike' was first used to describe the Honda CB750 of the late 1960s. Superbikes are designed for high-speed racing but can also be used for touring on public highways.

Ducati superbike

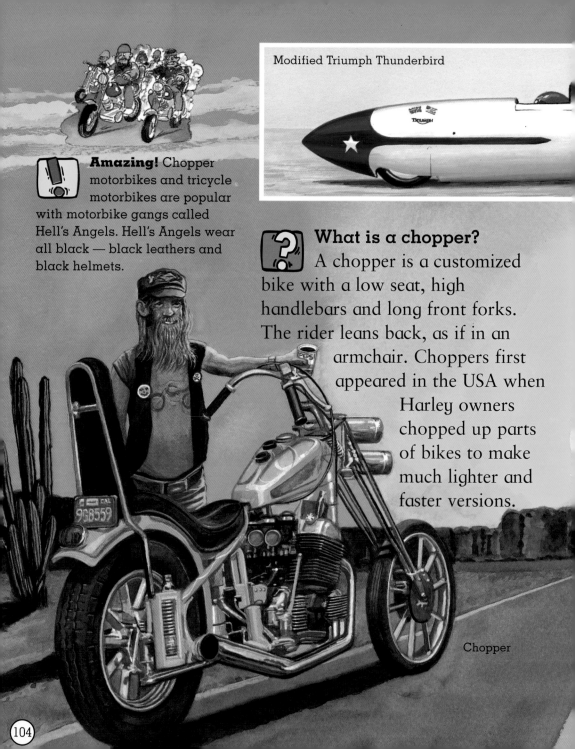

Modified Triumph Thunderbird

Amazing! Chopper motorbikes and tricycle motorbikes are popular with motorbike gangs called Hell's Angels. Hell's Angels wear all black — black leathers and black helmets.

What is a chopper?
A chopper is a customized bike with a low seat, high handlebars and long front forks. The rider leans back, as if in an armchair. Choppers first appeared in the USA when Harley owners chopped up parts of bikes to make much lighter and faster versions.

Chopper

 ## Who reached 214 mph on a Triumph?

Johnny Allen rode a cigar-shaped Triumph bike at 214 mph across the Bonneville Salt Flats in America in 1956. Triumph named their most famous bike the Bonneville after this feat.

 ### Is it true?
Chopped scooters are used for drag racing.

Yes. A drag race is a race between two motorbikes along a short, straight track. Some drag racers compete on chopped scooters, which are scooters with a beefed up engine and a long frame.

Who put three engines on a motorbike?
Russ Collins put three engines on to his Honda drag racer in the 1970s. Drag bikes need a huge amount of power for maximum acceleration, and some models are even powered by rocket engines!

Russ Collins

What is stunt riding?

Stunt riders speed up ramps on their bikes, and jump over cars, buses and trucks. The most famous stunt rider of all, Evel Knievel, even tried to jump a canyon in a rocket-powered 'skycycle' in 1974. He nearly drowned in the attempt. Evel claims that he has broken every bone in his body!

Evel Knievel

Amazing! Teams of stunt riders perform incredible tricks such as building motorbike pyramids and jumping through rings of fire. For a pyramid, the team members balance on each other's shoulders while the bikes are moving.

Wall of death

What is the wall of death?

The wall of death is a circular, vertical wall. Stunt riders whizz round and round it on their motorbikes, as if they're riding inside a tin can! They have to ride at full speed to stop falling off the wall.

 ## What is freestyle motocross?

Freestyle motocross is a new motorbike sport where the riders perform daring tricks as they jump off humps on a dirt track. Sometimes they even let go of their bikes completely!

 Is it true?
Riding on one wheel is impossible.

No. Riders can lift their front wheels off the ground and ride along on the rear wheel. This trick is called a wheelie. Superbike racers do wheelies to celebrate winning a race.

Freestyle motocross

107

CHAPTER SIX
TRUCKS AND DIGGERS

Which trucks had steam engines?

In the 19th century, the first powered trucks had steam engines, before gas engines and diesel engines were invented. They looked like the steam tractors used on farms.

Foden steam truck

Amazing! The first ever steam-powered vehicle was destroyed in a crash. The three-wheeled carriage was built by French engineer Nicolas-Joseph Cugnot in 1769, and was supposed to pull artillery guns.

What did trucks look like before steam engines were invented?

Before steam engines were invented, cargo was moved in wagons pulled by animals such as oxen or horses. This is why the first powered trucks and cars were called 'horseless' carriages.

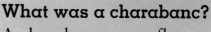

What was a charabanc?

A charabanc was a flat-bodied truck with benches in the back for passengers to sit on. Factory workers and their families traveled in charabancs on days out to the seaside or to the city. The first charabancs were pulled by teams of horses.

Is it true?

Early buses were pulled by steam tractors.

Yes. A steam tractor was a steam-powered vehicle designed for towing wagons. The first passenger-carrying buses were made up of a wagon with several seats inside, pulled by a steam tractor.

Charabanc

Wagon train

How do truck drivers talk to each other?

Truck drivers talk to each other on citizens' band (C.B.) radios. They warn each other about traffic jams or bad weather. Drivers use nicknames called handles instead of their real names.

 Amazing! During the winter, some truck drivers build fires under their cabs while they are stopped! When diesel fuel gets very cold it goes thick and gooey, so drivers try to keep it warm and runny so that their engines will start again without any trouble.

Trucker using CB radio

 Is it true?
Trucks have up to 16 gears.

Yes. Trucks need lots of gears. They need very low gears for starting off with a heavy load and for slowly climbing steep hills. They also need very high gears for traveling quickly on highways.

Sleeper compartment

Where do truckers sleep?

Some long-distance truck drivers sleep in bunks behind or over their seats. The biggest trucks have a sleeper compartment behind the cab, with a bathroom and shower.

Jack-knifed truck

What is a jack-knife?

A jack-knife happens when a truck driver tries to stop, but the trailer slides sideways, out of control. A jack-knife is very dangerous – the trailer might turn over. It is named after a knife with a folding blade.

What is a monster truck?

A monster truck is an ordinary pick-up truck fitted with huge dump-truck wheels, extra-strong suspension and a very powerful engine. Monster truck owners race their trucks over tracks with huge bumps and jumps. The trucks bounce about and even tip over if they go too quickly.

Monster truck

Is it true?
Monster trucks drive over cars.

Yes. In monster truck racing, some of the obstacles that the trucks drive over are old cars! The cars get crushed flat under the trucks' massive wheels.

Bedford Afghan truck

Who paints trucks for protection?

In countries such as Afghanistan and India, truck drivers paint their trucks with bright colors and religious symbols. They believe that the symbols will stop them from having accidents.

Customized pick-up truck

What are customized trucks?

Customized trucks have special parts such as huge wheels, high suspensions and big engines. Some even have trunks, bonnets and doors moved by hydraulic rams. Custom trucks are built specially for shows and races.

Amazing! One of most famous American monster trucks is called Grave Digger. It has an amazing custom paint job, with scenes of graveyards all over its bodywork!

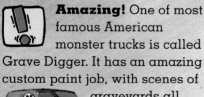

115

How do tanks travel?

Tanks are good at driving across rough, muddy ground, but they're quite slow. When tanks need to move quickly, they're carried on special tank transporters. The transporter's trailer needs lots of wheels to spread out the huge weight of the tank.

Oshkosh tank transporter

Amphibious trucks

Which trucks can swim?

Armies transport equipment in amphibious trucks that can drive on land like a normal truck and float across water like a boat. Amphibious trucks have a waterproof underside to stop water flooding the engine.

Amazing! Some trucks have armor plating on the outside. They're called armored personnel carriers (APCs for short). They're used to carry troops on battlefields.

What carries missiles?

Missile-carrying trucks transport huge nuclear missiles. On board the truck is a launch pad and a control center for launching the missile. The trucks carry the missiles into the countryside if their base is threatened by enemy attack.

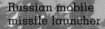
Russian mobile missile launcher

Is it true?
Some trucks have caterpillar tracks.

Yes. A type of truck called a half-track has wheels at the front and caterpillar tracks at the rear. Armies often transport their troops in half-tracks.

Is it true?
Some trucks have bullet-proof glass.

Yes. Demolition machines have extra-strong, bullet-proof glass in their cabs. The glass stops falling masonry crashing into the cab and hurting the driver.

Which digger can do different jobs?

A type of digger called a backhoe loader can dig, load and drill. At the back is a digger arm with a bucket called a backhoe. At the front is a shovel for picking up loose soil and rock. Different sized buckets or a pneumatic drill can be attached to the backhoe.

Backhoe loader

Amazing! There are mini digging machines as well as big ones. Mini machines are used where large machines can't go, such as in basements, and for digging small trenches in sidewalks and yards.

118

Mobile crane

Which trucks can reach high up?

A mobile crane is a truck with a crane on its back. Mobiles cranes work on construction sites, lifting heavy objects such as steel girders into place with their telescopic arms. There is a cab at the back for the driver who operates the crane.

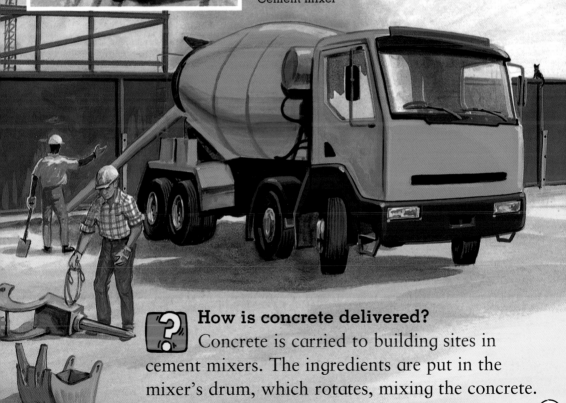

Cement mixer

How is concrete delivered?

Concrete is carried to building sites in cement mixers. The ingredients are put in the mixer's drum, which rotates, mixing the concrete.

What are chains used for?

Strong metal chains called snow chains stop trucks skidding on icy or snow-covered highways. The chains are wrapped around all the truck's tires and cut into the ice or snow, gripping it tightly. In cold countries, truck drivers always carry snow chains with them.

Scania six-wheeler

Snow chains

Amazing! Some farm tractors have huge double sets of wheels to stop them from churning up the soil. In very muddy ground, normal tractors sink into the mud. Double wheels spread the tractor's weight over a bigger area to stop it sinking.

DAF Turbotwin rally truck

 Which trucks race across the Sahara?

Trucks compete in many rallies, including the famous Paris-Dakar Rally that crosses the Sahara Desert in northern Africa. More trucks carry spares and mechanics for other competitors, who race in cars and on motorbikes.

Four-wheel drive pick up truck

What is four-wheel drive?

When a truck has four-wheel drive, it means that the engine makes all the wheels turn. In some trucks, the engine only turns two of the wheels. Four-wheel drive is good for driving off-road on muddy tracks.

Which fire truck has two drivers?

Some fire trucks carry ladders so long that the ladder needs its own extra-long trailer. A second driver in a rear cab turns the rear wheels of the trailer so that the truck can get round sharp corners to reach fires in narrow streets.

Amazing! Water is pumped along fire hoses by a powerful pump in a fire truck. It comes out of the hose nozzle so quickly that the fire fighter holding the nozzle can be lifted off the ground.

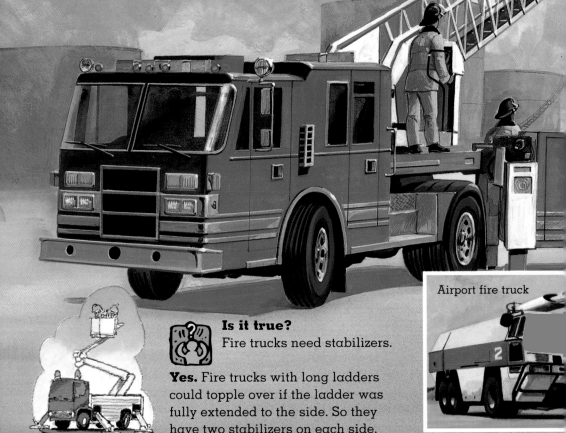

Airport fire truck

Is it true?
Fire trucks need stabilizers.

Yes. Fire trucks with long ladders could topple over if the ladder was fully extended to the side. So they have two stabilizers on each side.

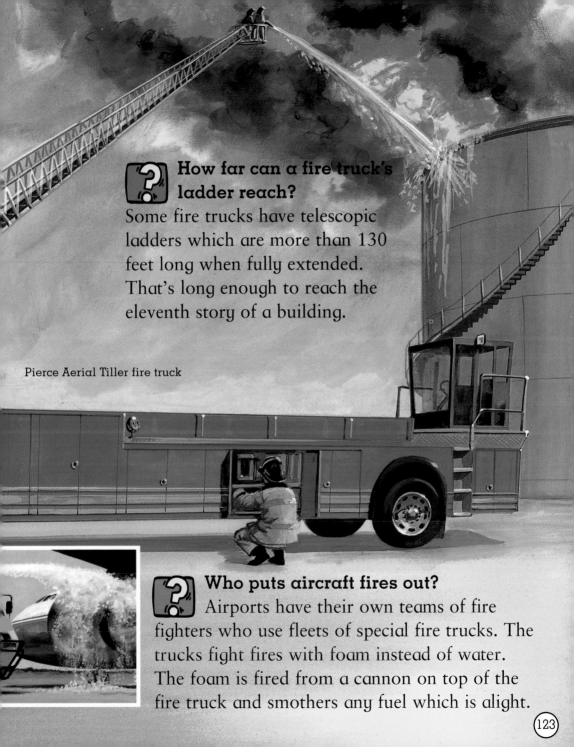

How far can a fire truck's ladder reach?

Some fire trucks have telescopic ladders which are more than 130 feet long when fully extended. That's long enough to reach the eleventh story of a building.

Pierce Aerial Tiller fire truck

Who puts aircraft fires out?

Airports have their own teams of fire fighters who use fleets of special fire trucks. The trucks fight fires with foam instead of water. The foam is fired from a cannon on top of the fire truck and smothers any fuel which is alight.

123

What is a wrecker?

A wrecker is a recovery truck that tows away cars, buses and other vehicles that are wrecked in accidents, often blocking highways or lying in ditches. Wreckers need powerful diesel engines for towing and a winch for pulling vehicles that have tipped over back on to their wheels.

Amazing! Some cargo trucks carry a mini fork-lift truck with them for loading and unloading cargo. The fork-lift folds up and is carried attached to the back of the main truck.

Wrecker

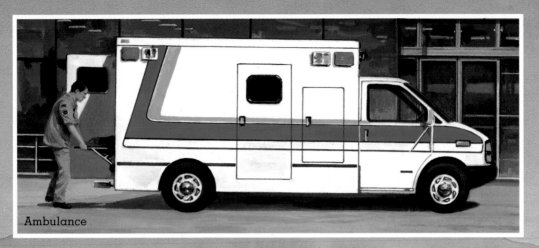

Ambulance

Which truck saves lives?

An ambulance is a small truck specially adapted to carry injured and sick people quickly to hospital. There are stretchers for patients and emergency medical equipment in the back of the ambulance.

Is it true?

Hospitals have wheels.

Yes. Mobile hospitals are mini hospitals inside a converted truck. They work in remote areas where people cannot get hospital treatment, and carry doctors, nurses and even an operating theater.

What needs a ramp to unload?

Tipper trucks have a lifting body that tips up to make a load slide out. Sometimes whole trucks are tipped up by a ramp instead! This truck is unloading grain into a grain store.

Grain truck unloading

Garbage truck

Which truck tows aircraft?

Airport tugs pull aircraft around when the aircraft cannot use their engines. The tug has a tow bar that attaches to an aircraft's front wheel. Its low body doesn't bump into the fuselage.

Is it true?
Cherry pickers are used to pick fruit.

No. Cherry picker is the nickname for a truck with a working platform on the end of an extending arm. A worker on the platform can do jobs such as changing bulbs in street lamps.

Airliner tug

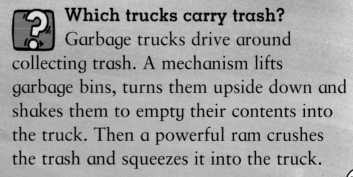

Which trucks carry trash?

Garbage trucks drive around collecting trash. A mechanism lifts garbage bins, turns them upside down and shakes them to empty their contents into the truck. Then a powerful ram crushes the trash and squeezes it into the truck.

CHAPTER SEVEN
AIRCRAFT

Who were the first people to fly?

The first people to make a proper flight were two Frenchmen, François Pilâtre de Rozier and the Marquis d'Arlandes. On November 21, 1783 they flew for 25 minutes over Paris in a hot-air balloon made by the Montgolfier brothers.

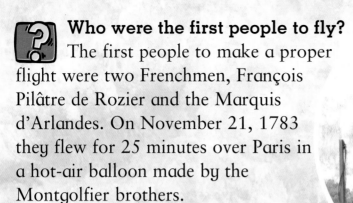

Montgolfier balloon

Who built a steam plane?

The first plane to leave the ground was the steam-powered Éole. It was built by French aviator Clément Ader, and had bat-like wings. It only flew for about 55 yards in 1890, and could not be steered!

Éole

 Amazing! In the 14th century Chinese merchants launched kites with people tied to them to see if it was windy enough to set sail in their ships. If the kite failed to fly, they stayed in port until another day. This fact was reported by the famous European traveler Marco Polo.

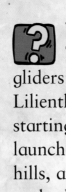 ## Who flew the first gliders?

The first person to build and fly gliders was the German engineer Otto Lilienthal. He made hundreds of flights, starting in 1891. Lilienthal launched himself from hills, and hung under his gliders. He was killed in a glider crash in 1896.

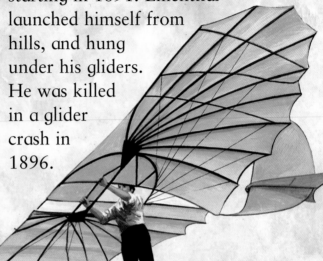

Otto Lilienthal

Is it true?
People flew by flapping their arms.

No. For hundreds of years people attempted to fly by strapping wings to their arms and flapping them. They became known as 'birdmen', and many were injured or killed, after they launched themselves from high buildings or cliffs. For humans, flying like birds is impossible because we do not have shoulder muscles which are strong enough for flapping.

Who made the first airplane flight?

The first person to make a controlled flight in an airplane with an engine was Orville Wright. His flight took place in the airplane Flyer on December 17, 1903 at Kitty Hawk, North Carolina, USA. The flight lasted just 12 seconds and was 40 yards long. Flyer was a biplane built by Orville and his brother Wilbur, who were bicycle makers.

Antoinette monoplane

Flyer

Amazing! In 1914, the fastest aircraft were slower than the fastest racing cars. The world speed record for aircraft was just over 126 miles per hour, but the world land-speed record was 140 miles per hour. By 1920, aircraft had overtaken.

What is a monoplane?

A monoplane is a plane with one pair of wings. Most early planes were biplanes, with two sets of wings. The graceful Antoinette VII of 1908 was one of the first monoplanes to fly.

Is it true?

One plane had 20 wings.

Yes. In 1904 Englishman Horatio Phillips built a plane with 20 small wings one above the other. It was a complete failure. In 1907 he built a plane with no less than 200 wings!

Blériot XI

Who was first to fly across the English Channel?

The first cross-channel flight was made by Frenchman Louis Blériot in 1909. He made the trip in one of his own airplanes, a Blériot number XI monoplane. It took just 37 minutes to fly from France to England. Blériot won a prize of £1,000.

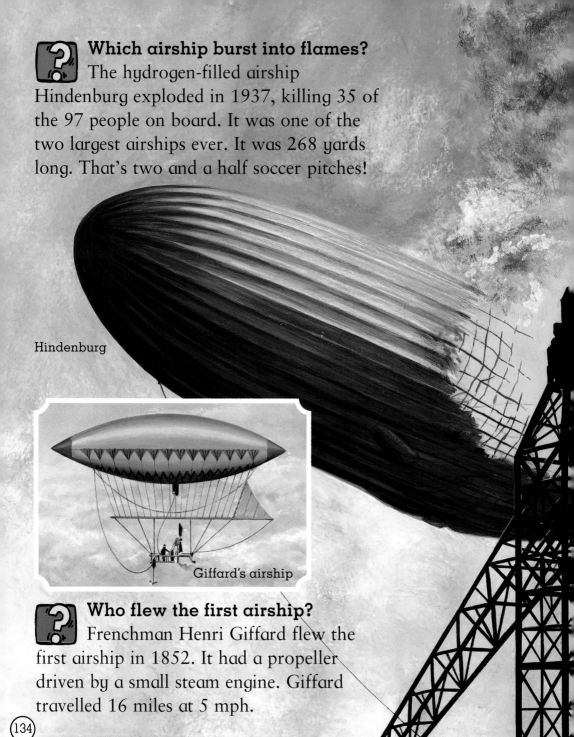

Which airship burst into flames?

The hydrogen-filled airship Hindenburg exploded in 1937, killing 35 of the 97 people on board. It was one of the two largest airships ever. It was 268 yards long. That's two and a half soccer pitches!

Hindenburg

Giffard's airship

Who flew the first airship?

Frenchman Henri Giffard flew the first airship in 1852. It had a propeller driven by a small steam engine. Giffard travelled 16 miles at 5 mph.

Amazing!
In 1802 Frenchman André Jacques Garnerin jumped from the basket of his hot-air balloon above London. He floated safely down under a parachute. It was the first successful parachute jump.

Breitling Orbiter

 Is it true?
The first non-stop round-the-world balloon flight was in 1999.

Yes. Bertrand Piccard and Brian Jones flew the Breitling Orbiter 3 from Chateaux D'Oex in Switzerland, and crossed the finishing line in Mauritania 19 days, 21 hours and 55 minutes later. Piccard and Jones finally landed in the Egyptian desert.

Are airships used today?
Today small airships fly above major sporting events. They carry television cameras to give viewers a bird's eye view of the action. They often have huge advertising displays on their sides.

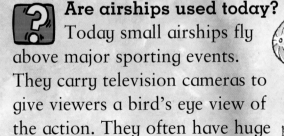

Ryan M2 monoplane
'Spirit of St Louis'

Who made the first solo flight across the Atlantic?

American pilot Charles Lindbergh made the first non-stop transatlantic solo flight in 1927. His all-metal Ryan monoplane, called Spirit of St Louis, was built specially for the job. The flight took 33 hours and 30 minutes. Lindbergh tried to stay awake all the time to avoid crashing into the sea.

Amazing! US Navy airman Richard E Byrd was the first man to fly over both the North Pole and the South Pole. He reached the North Pole in May 1926 as navigator in a Fokker F.VIIA and the South Pole in November 1929 as commander of a Ford tri-motor.

Who was first to fly across the Pacific?

In 1928, Australians Charles Kingsford Smith, Charles Ulm and their navigators made the first flight from America to Australia in a Fokker tri-motor. They refueled four times on Pacific islands.

Fokker tri-motor

 Is it true?
The first solo airplane flight around the world took nearly eight days.

Yes. The first round-the-world solo flight was made between July 15 and 22, 1933. Total flying time was 7 days, 18 hours and 49 minutes for the 15,560 miles. The pilot was an American called Wiley Post, and his aircraft was a Lockheed Vega.

Which woman flew solo from England to Australia?

English pilot Amy Johnson made the first solo England-Australia flight by a woman, in a Gypsy Moth biplane in 1930. She had many near disasters on the way, including almost flying into a mountain side.

Gypsy Moth

Amy Johnson

Surface-effect vehicle

Is it true?
Some seaplanes fly just above the waves.

Yes. Experimental seaplanes called surface-effect vehicles fly very close to the water surface. Air squashed between their wings and the water helps to keep the plane flying. It means that the wings can be smaller than those on normal planes of the same size.

Which plane is also a boat?
A flying boat is a plane with a fuselage shaped like the hull of a boat. It takes off and lands on water instead of a runway. During the 1930s huge flying boats such as the Short C-class Empire were popular for traveling long distances.

Amazing! In 1938, a seaplane was carried into the air by a flying boat. The seaplane did not use any fuel to take off and so was able fly non-stop across the Atlantic.

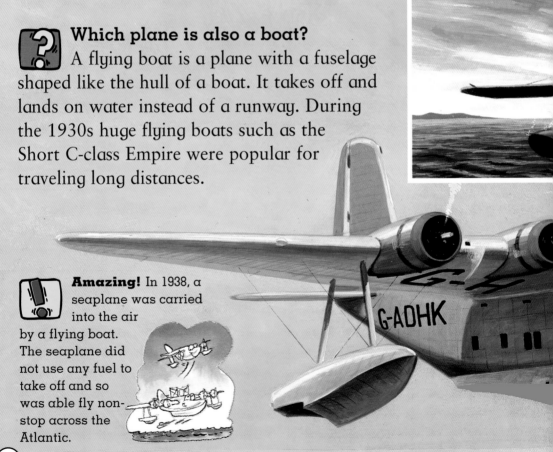

G-ADHK

How fast could seaplanes go?

In 1931, a Supermarine seaplane set a new world speed record, and won the Schneider Trophy. It was powered by a special Rolls Royce engine, and reached 406 mph!

 ## How do planes land on snow?

Planes can land on a flat stretch of snow or ice if they change their wheeled undercarriage for skis. One of the first planes with skis was a Fokker F.VIIA used to fly over the North Pole. Modern ski planes take supplies to polar bases.

Supermarine S.6B

Short 'Maia' flying boat

Who invented the jet engine?

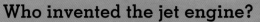

The jet engine was first thought of in 1930 by British engineer Frank Whittle. By 1937 he had built a working jet engine. At the same time in Germany Hans von Ohain was building a similar engine.

de Havilland Comet

S·ALVO

BOAC

Heinkel He 178

Amazing! When the first jet-powered plane took off on its maiden flight, it sucked a bird into its engine. The plane was the Heinkel He 178. All modern jet engines are designed to withstand 'bird strikes', which could snap off the engine's fan blades and cause a crash.

What was the first jet plane?

The first two jet planes were experimental fighters built during the Second World War. The German Heinkel He 178 flew in 1939 and the British Gloster E.28/39 in 1941.

Gloster E28/39

Is it true?

Jet engines have fans.

Yes. At the front of a jet engine there is an enormous fan which sucks in air. Large airliners have jet engines called turbofans, with fans as tall as a person. The fan compresses the air and forces it into the engine. Fuel burns in the air, creating a rush of hot gases which blast out of the engine. They spin a turbine that works the fan.

What was the first jet airliner?

The first jet airliner to carry passengers was the de Havilland Comet I. It had four jet engines set into the wing roots. The first airline service using the Comet was begun in 1952 by the British Overseas Airways Corporation, between London and Johannesburg.

Air pulled in and compressed by front fans

Exhaust provides thrust

Compressed air and fuel burnt in combustion chamber

Which is the biggest plane?

The biggest plane in the world is the six-engined Antonov An-225 transport airplane. It can carry other aircraft on its back as well as cargo inside. It can take off weighing a massive 600 tons.

Antonov An-225

Boeing 747 'Jumbo Jet'

 Which transatlantic airliner has only two engines?

The Boeing 777 flies across the Atlantic with only two engines. Before 1984, all transatlantic airliners had three or four engines in case one failed. Now, engines are more reliable.

Amazing! One gigantic flying boat with eight engines, the Hughes H4 Hercules, measured nearly 110 yards from one wing tip to the other and could have carried 700 passengers! Nicknamed 'Spruce Goose', it only flew once in 1947 and is now in a museum.

Is it true?
Some planes carry tanks.

Yes. Monster military transport planes like the Lockheed C5 Galaxy and Antonov An-124 are big enough for tanks. The Galaxy can lift two 50-ton tanks, which drive in up ramps in the nose or tail.

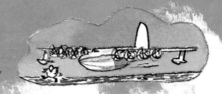

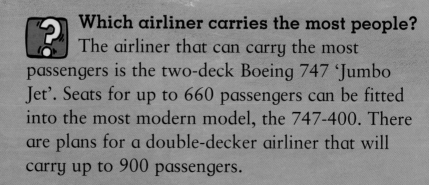

Which airliner carries the most people?
The airliner that can carry the most passengers is the two-deck Boeing 747 'Jumbo Jet'. Seats for up to 660 passengers can be fitted into the most modern model, the 747-400. There are plans for a double-decker airliner that will carry up to 900 passengers.

Which plane traveled at 4,500 miles per hour?

On October 3, 1967 an American X-15 rocket-powered airplane reached 4,500 mph. It's still the world record speed for an airplane. The X-15 also holds the altitude record of 354,200 feet. That's nearly 67 miles above the Earth's surface!

X-15 rocket plane

Which plane had no wings?

In the 1970s, US Air Force pilots flew an experimental plane called the X-24A without wings. This rocket plane had a specially shaped fuselage, or lifting body, to keep airborne.

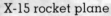

Lockheed SR-71A
'Blackbird'

Is it true?
You can travel faster than the speed of sound.

Yes. Some supersonic planes with powerful engines, like Concorde, can fly faster than sound. Sound travels at about 750 mph.

Amazing! The famous American fighter ace and test pilot Chuck Yeager was the first person to fly faster than the speed of sound (Mach 1). In 1947 he flew the rocket-powered Bell X-1 to Mach 1.015.

Bell X-1

Chuck Yeager

Which is the fastest jet?
The fastest jet aircraft ever was the American Lockheed SR-71A 'Blackbird' spy plane. It holds the official speed record of an incredible 2193.17 mph, which it set in 1976. In 1974 it set the New York to London record time of 1 hour and 55 minutes.

Which jet plane can hover?

The Harrier attack aircraft can take off and land vertically and also hover in the air. The exhaust from its jet engines comes out of four swiveling nozzles. For hovering, the nozzles point downwards. For forward flight, they point backwards.

Harrier attack aircraft

Amazing! Engineers built a bizarre machine nicknamed the 'Flying Bedstead' to test vertical take-off and landing aircraft. It had two jet engines, and its real name was the Thrust Measuring Rig.

de Havilland Dash

Which planes can take off and land in cities?

The de Havilland Dash flies between small airports with short runways that are often near city centers. The Dash can take off and land on a runway only a few hundred yards long.

Which plane can swivel its engines?

The Bell/Boeing V-22 Osprey is part helicopter, part plane. It has propellers or proprotors, which swivel upright for take-off, and it works like a helicopter. To go forwards, they swivel down and it flies like a plane.

Bell/Boeing V-22

Is it true?
People can fly with jet-packs.

Yes. By strapping on the Bell rocket belt, a pilot could take off and hover in the air. At the beginning of the film Thunderball, James Bond escapes from his enemies with one. However the amount of fuel stored in the rocket belt limits the flying time to less than 30 seconds.

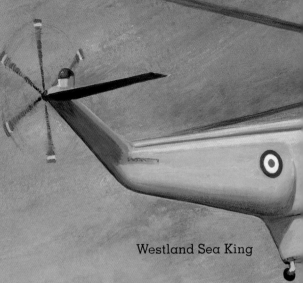

 Why are helicopters used for rescuing people?

Helicopters make good rescue aircraft because they can hover in the air and land in small spaces. At sea they hover while the crew pull people from the water. They are also used to lift injured mountaineers to hospital.

Westland Sea King

Sikorsky VS-300

 Amazing! Helicopters can be used as cranes! 'Skycranes' can move heavy objects over short distances. They have a cargo space where the fuselage normally is.

 Who invented the first true helicopter?

People had been making brief helicopter flights since 1907, but the first successful helicopter flight was in 1939. Inventor Igor Sikorsky flew his VS-300, which had a single main rotor and a tail rotor. This was the ancestor of all modern helicopters.

No. Very modern helicopters have a tail thruster, instead of a second rotor, but most helicopters do have two rotors. As the engine spins the main rotor one way, it also tries to spin the fuselage the other way. A second rotor on the tail stops this happening. On twin-rotor helicopters, the main rotors spin in opposite directions, so no tail rotor is needed.

Autogyro

What is an autogyro?

An autogyro has a rotor that is not driven by an engine. As the autogyro is pushed along by its propeller, the rotor spins round automatically, providing the lift that keeps the autogyro in the air.

CHAPTER EIGHT
SPACECRAFT

Who made the first liquid fuel rocket?

Robert Goddard, an American engineer, launched the first liquid fuel rocket in March 1926. His rocket, burning petrol and liquid oxygen, flew to a height of 40 feet and landed 184 feet from the launch pad. He showed that space flight might be possible in the future.

Robert Goddard

Amazing! The Chinese invented rockets around the beginning of the last millennium! Powered by an early version of gunpowder, Chinese rockets in AD 1000 looked like fireworks. They were used in battle as flaming arrows! For the last 1,000 years, most big advances in rocket design have been made as a result of war.

What did the first satellite do?

Sputnik 1 was launched into orbit by Soviet Russia on October 4, 1957, 121 days ahead of its American rival, Explorer 1. Sputnik circled the Earth once every 90 minutes, sending radio messages for 21 days, which the world listened to on the radio.

Sputnik

German V2 Rocket

 ### Is it true?

Rockets were used in World War 2.

Yes. The German scientist Wernher von Braun made rockets that could launch bombs across the English Channel. They damaged London without risking the lives of German pilots. Von Braun's V2 rocket was so successful that after the war, America gave him a job helping with its space program.

 ## Who was the first earthling in space?

Before the first humans went to space, animals paved the way. Laika, a Russian mongrel dog, was the first earthling in space. Her seven days in orbit proved that space travel would be safe for humans.

Laika

What was the biggest rocket ever?

Saturn 5

American Saturn 5 rockets were 364 feet tall monsters, weighing 2,903 tons on the launch pad. That's as heavy as 600 elephants! They were more greedy than elephants, too, burning 15 tons of fuel per second. Saturn 5 rockets were used to launch all the Apollo missions to the Moon.

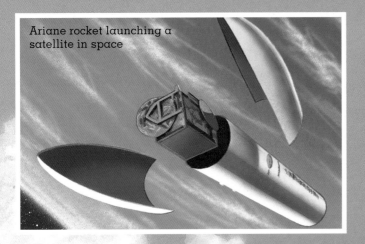

Ariane rocket launching a satellite in space

What do rockets carry?

Rocket cargo is called the payload, the load that pays for the trip. Most rockets are designed to carry one or two satellites. Some satellites are for scientific research, some are for communication, and some are for spying. Of course, rockets can also carry people!

No. Jet engines need to take oxygen from the air around them to burn fuel. Because there's no air in space, a jet engine wouldn't work up there.

Why do rockets have stages?

Rockets have to be big to carry enough fuel to escape the Earth's pull. But once the fuel is burnt, those big engines and fuel tanks are useless. Their weight would make visiting the Moon very difficult. So rockets are made in stages, or pieces, which drop off when they've done their job.

Amazing! Three German engineers made a rocket-powered car in 1928! Fritz von Opel, Max Valier and Friedrich Sander tested the first version, Opel-Rak 1, on March 15, 1928. Opel later used the rocket knowledge he learnt from Valier to fit 16 rockets on to a glider plane. It was the second ever rocket-powered aircraft.

Launch escape system

Command module

Service module

Lunar module inside

Stage 3 contains fuel and rocket engines

Stage 2 contains fuel and rocket engines

Stage 1 contains fuel and rocket engines

Saturn 5

Which spacecraft is reusable?

The space shuttle was the world's first reusable spacecraft. Instead of a stack of rocket stages, it has separate booster rockets and a big fuel tank. The shuttle drops these before reaching orbit. It eventually glides back to Earth using its wings.

3

3 Eventually the shuttle returns to Earth to be used again.

2

2 The fuel tank is jettisoned and burns up in the atmosphere. This is the only part that isn't reused.

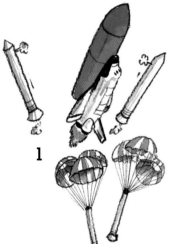

1

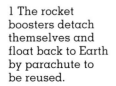

1 The rocket boosters detach themselves and float back to Earth by parachute to be reused.

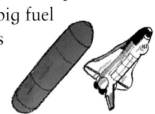

MMU in action

What is an MMU?

The Manned Maneuvring Unit, or MMU, is a small strap-on spacecraft. Together with a space suit, the MMU lets an astronaut move freely through space. It uses 24 tiny jets of gas to travel in any direction.

Amazing! The shuttle has a special area for cargo. It can hold up to 29 tons. That's the size and weight of an adult humpback whale!

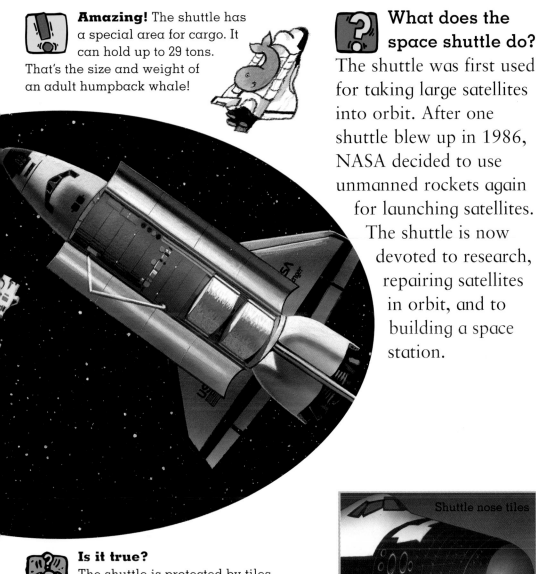

What does the space shuttle do?

The shuttle was first used for taking large satellites into orbit. After one shuttle blew up in 1986, NASA decided to use unmanned rockets again for launching satellites. The shuttle is now devoted to research, repairing satellites in orbit, and to building a space station.

Is it true?
The shuttle is protected by tiles.

Yes. The shuttle is made from aluminum. This metal is very light, but it melts at high temperatures. A shuttle can heat up to 6,360° as it returns to Earth, so it needs 20,000 heat proof tiles, which are glued on to its nose and belly.

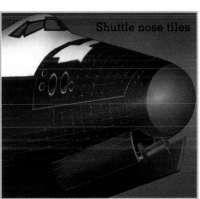

Shuttle nose tiles

What is a satellite?

Anything in orbit around the world is a satellite. Man-made satellites are normally smaller than a car. People make satellites for special jobs. Some study the Earth, some bounce electronic messages around the world, and some are telescopes for studying the universe. Earth has a natural satellite, too – the Moon.

Communications satellite

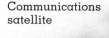
Pull of Earth's gravity stops satellite flying off

Orbital path of satellite

How do satellites stay up?

Once satellites have been launched by rocket, they try to zoom off into space, while the Earth tries to pull them down. The two movements added together balance out, making the satellite travel in a circle, called the orbital path.

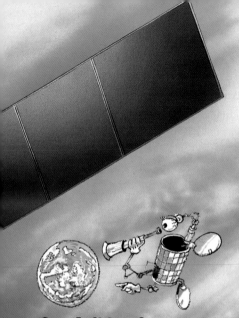

Do satellites ever fall out of the sky?

Yes, accidents can happen! Satellites have crashed into the ocean, and pieces of the empty space station, Skylab, were found on farmland in Australia, after it fell back to Earth in 1979.

Satellite crashing into the ocean

Is it true?

There are spy satellites in the sky.

Yes. A big reason for the space race between Russia and America was to spy on each other. Spy satellites use telescopic cameras. Early spy satellites used to drop films to Earth by parachute. Now they take digital photos and beam them home, using secret codes.

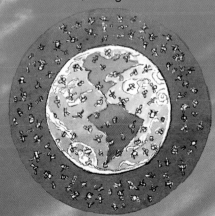

Amazing! There are 150,000 bits of space garbage! They fly at incredible speeds, making them very dangerous. A window on a space shuttle was chipped once by a collision with a flake of paint! The American air force keeps track of the largest 8,500 objects in orbit. Letting trash drop and burn-up in the atmosphere helps to clean up space.

 ## Is there a telescope in space?

Astronomers on Earth have their view spoilt by our cloudy, dirty atmosphere, which makes stars seem to twinkle. There is no air in space, so distant objects are much clearer. The Hubble Space Telescope has taken photos of galaxies 13 billion light years away!

Amazing! You can join space telescopes together to make one huge eye in the sky! First, lots of small space telescopes have to be launched into space. Then they need to line up, like beads on a very big necklace. Computers compare what each telescope can see, and fill in the gaps. This can make a virtual telescope as big as a city!

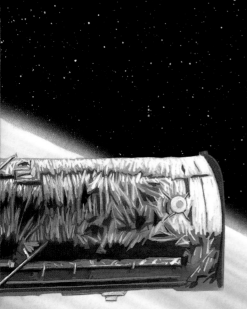

Hubble telescope

Repairing Hubble

Is it true?
The Hubble telescope can see stars being born.

Yes. The Hubble image here shows stars being made in the Eagle Nebula. The fingers of cloud are bigger than our entire solar system. They are made of gas and dust, which slowly collects into lumps. As they grow, the lumps become hotter, creating thousands of new stars!

Eagle Nebula

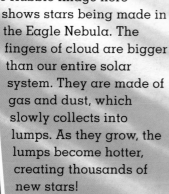

What happens if the telescope breaks down?

Hubble had to be fixed by astronauts almost as soon as it was launched. The mirror it uses to collect images was the wrong shape, making pictures fuzzy. In December 1993 a shuttle met up with Hubble, and astronauts adjusted the mirror successfully.

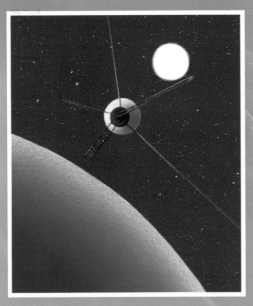

 Which voyagers visited all the planets?

Humans can't travel to other planets yet. A trip to Mars would need much bigger spacecraft than the shuttle. Instead, unmanned space probes like Voyager can travel through the solar system, sending home pictures of the planets.

Voyager probe passing Neptune

 Is it true?
A Mariner took photos of Mercury.

Yes. A very successful space probe called Mariner 10 visited the planet Mercury three times in the 1970s. As well as taking photos, Mariner discovered Mercury's strange magnetic field, and signs of ice at the poles.

Venera probe

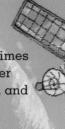 **Which probe got too hot?**

Four Venera probes have landed on Venus. The temperature there is a sweaty 1020°. As if that wasn't nasty enough, the clouds rain pure sulphuric acid!

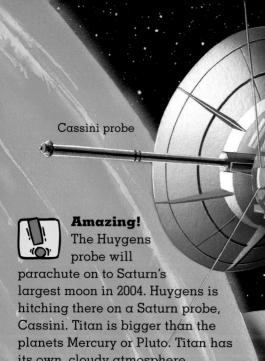

Cassini probe

 Amazing!
The Huygens probe will parachute on to Saturn's largest moon in 2004. Huygens is hitching there on a Saturn probe, Cassini. Titan is bigger than the planets Mercury or Pluto. Titan has its own, cloudy atmosphere, blocking our view of its surface. Titan might be covered in an ocean, so Huygens is designed to float!

Which probe visited a comet?

Giotto was made to visit Halley's Comet as it passed Earth in 1986. Giotto had a special shield to protect it from the dust of the comet's tail. The probe took measurements and photographs from 370 miles away, revealing the rocky heart of the comet.

Giotto passing Halley's Comet

Is it true?
There is life on Mars.

No. Probes have tested Martian soil for life. They added food to the soil to see if there was anything living there that was hungry! There wasn't. Then scientists found what looked like fossils inside a rock from Mars. After careful checking, they decided that the shapes were probably odd looking crystals. So there is no life on Mars, unless it is very good at hiding from us!

What bounced around on Mars?

The Mars Pathfinder probe dropped on to Mars inside a bundle of balloons. The balloons bounced away from the falling parachute, deflated, then the Sojourner rover slowly drove away over them.

Mars Pathfinder landing

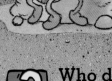

Who drove a vehicle on Mars?

The Mars Pathfinder (1997) had a small, six-wheeled rover, called Sojourner. It used a camera and laser beams to find its way. Scientists on Earth asked Sojourner to examine particular objects, by radio. But the robot car had to decide how to reach them.

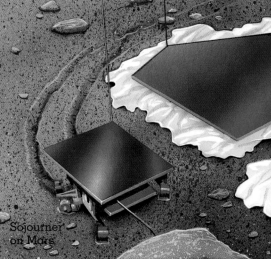

Sojourner on Mars

Did Vikings really land on Mars?

Two space probes, called Viking 1 and Viking 2, landed on Mars in the 1970s. They took 3,000 photos, some in 3-D, and beamed them back to Earth. The Viking probes also measured weather patterns and examined the soil for signs of life. They didn't find any aliens.

Mars probe

Amazing! For 20 years before Pathfinder, several probes sent to Mars ended in disaster. Sixteen probes from Russia either exploded on launch, missed the planet, or crashed into its surface. The American probe Observer exploded as it entered Mars's orbit. Some probes just went missing. Nobody knows why.

Who is building a new space station?

America is leading a group of countries to build an international space station (ISS). The space shuttle is used to deliver parts. Most are made in America, but there are Japanese, Russian, Canadian and European parts as well. ISS uses giant solar panels to make its own electricity.

John Glenn

Amazing! John Glenn went to space at the age of 77. Sensors on his skin were used to monitor his health. His record-breaking flight happened 36 years after his first space trip, when he was the first American to orbit the Earth.

International space station

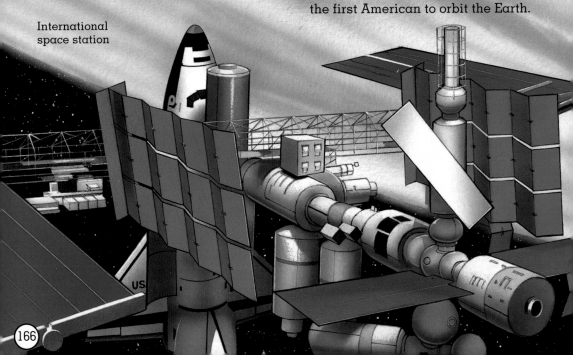

Will there ever be a Moon Base?

If space gets a lot busier it will make sense to use the Moon as a base. The Moon's low gravity lets big spacecraft take off and land easily compared to Earth.

Future Moon base

 Is it true?
People can be 'buried' in space.

Yes. A cheap new rocket called Pegasus has made space funerals possible. The rocket delivered 25 people's ashes into space in 1997. For under $5,000 each, the ashes were scattered in orbit. They will drift back to Earth after a few years.

 ## Will I ever go to space?

Only a few people become astronauts. But tourists may soon be able to holiday in space. There are plans to use empty shuttle fuel tanks as the rooms of a space hotel!

Space hotel of the future

 What will spacecraft be like in the future?

Space shuttles will be replaced quite soon with space planes. America is developing a space plane called VentureStar. It could cost 70% less to fly than the shuttle. VentureStars could make it possible to reach orbit cheaply, and even to build other ships in space. Then we could make giant transporter ships to carry people to Mars.

VentureStar

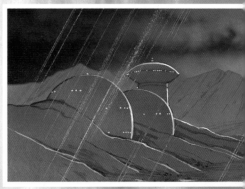

Will we ever visit other solar systems?

The nearest star to our Sun is 4.3 light years away. The shuttle would take 158,000 years to get there! We will need amazing new spacecraft before we visit other solar systems.

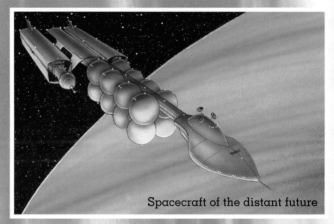

Spacecraft of the distant future

Amazing! You might travel to space on a laser beam! Scientists in America are testing a laser that heats a pocket of air under a spacecraft. The very hot air pushes the craft upwards. No energy is wasted lifting heavy fuel off the ground.

Will we colonise Mars?

Robots might be able to build a Mars base. Humans would have to wear space suits outside, but would live in airtight habitats, with plants and animals. Genetically modified plants could grow, which would create breathable air and water, making the whole planet habitable.

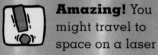
Colonizing Mars

CHAPTER NINE
DINOSAURS
AND OTHER PREHISTORIC REPTILES

 What were the dinosaurs?

Dinosaurs were reptiles of many amazing shapes and sizes that lived long ago. They had just the same needs as the animals you know today – to hunt, feed, breed and escape their enemies.

Triassic   Jurassic

Herrerasaurus

 Is it true?
Dinosaurs only lived on land.

Yes. They were adapted for life on land because they walked with straight legs tucked underneath their bodies, as we do. This gave them an advantage over other animals and helped them dominate the land.

Where did they live?

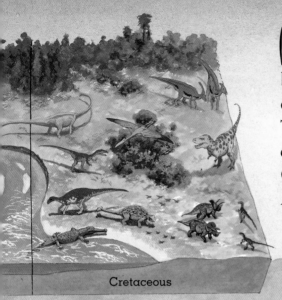

Cretaceous

Everywhere on Earth, but the planet was completely different in dinosaur times. The seas, plants, animals and continents, Laurasia and Gondwana, were all different. And there were no people!

Laurasia

Gondwana

When did they live?

Dinosaurs ruled the world for millions of years. They appeared about 225 million years ago and died out 65 million years ago. There were three periods in dinosaur history: Triassic, when the first dinosaurs appeared; Jurassic and Cretaceous, when dinosaurs dominated the land.

Amazing! One of the earliest dinosaurs ever found was Eoraptor, 'dawn stealer', and it lived 225 million years ago. It was only three feet long and probably a fierce hunter of small reptiles.

Eoraptor

Were there any other animals?

Insects, small mammals and many modern forms of life lived in the shadow of the dinosaurs, as well as other reptiles. Pterosaurs soared through the air, while Ichthyosaurs and Plesiosaurs swam in the seas.

Pterosaurs

Plesiosaur

Ichthyosaur

Where did dinosaurs come from?

There was life on Earth for over 3,000 million years before the dinosaurs. Mammal-like reptiles were living on the land just before the dinosaurs appeared. Some scientists think Lagosuchus (which means rabbit crocodile) was the ancestor of all dinosaurs.

Lagosuchus

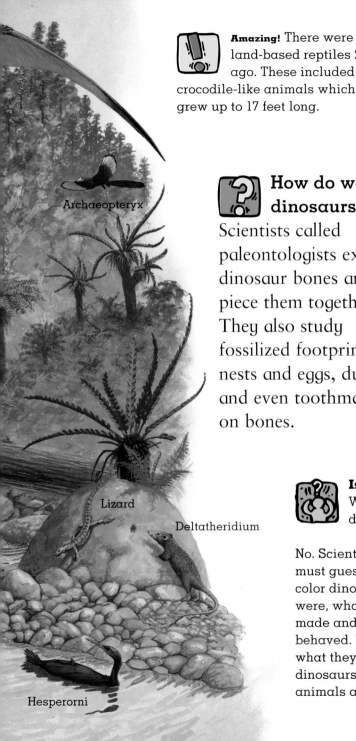

Amazing! There were many groups of land-based reptiles 245 million years ago. These included crocodile-like animals which grew up to 17 feet long.

How do we know that dinosaurs existed?

Scientists called paleontologists examine dinosaur bones and piece them together. They also study fossilized footprints, nests and eggs, dung and even toothmarks on bones.

Fossils

Archaeopteryx

Lizard

Deltatheridium

Hesperorni

Is it true?
We know everything about dinosaurs from fossils.

No. Scientists must guess what color dinosaurs were, what noises they made and how they behaved. They compare what they know about dinosaurs with the animals alive today.

(175)

Which were the biggest dinosaurs?

In the Jurassic age, giant plant eaters called sauropods became the largest animals to walk on Earth. One of them, Ultrasauros, may have been up to 100 feet long and about 60 feet high, which is as tall as a six story building!

Is it true?

All sauropods were huge and wide.

No. Sauropods were huge, but some were 'slim'. This helped when they walked through woods looking for food.

Which dinosaurs were the smallest?

Compsognathus was the size of a turkey and weighed about six pounds. It hunted insects and lizards. Heterodontosaurus and Lesothosaurus, both plant-eating dinosaurs, were just as small.

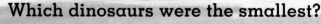
Compsognathus

Which were the heaviest dinosaurs?

Ultrasauros may have weighed as much as 50 tons, but scientists have recently found evidence of an even bigger dinosaur in Argentina. The gigantic Argentinosaurus may have weighed as much as 100 tons. Most sauropods were smaller, weighing between 30 and 80 tons.

Ultrasauros

Amazing! The neck of Mamenchisaurus was 50 feet long, strengthened by a system of spines. It could not have been lifted very high. Mamenchisaurus probably fed on low-growing vegetation.

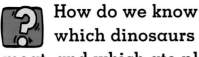 How do we know which dinosaurs ate meat, and which ate plants?

We can tell by looking at fossils of their teeth and claws. Meat-eaters and plant-eaters developed different special features, such as hands that could grasp and grinding or shearing teeth.

Plant eater fossil

Meat eater fossil

Yunnanosaurus

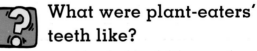 What were plant-eaters' teeth like?

Yunnanosaurus had chisel-like teeth to cut up tough vegetation. Some sauropods had spoon-shaped teeth for cutting tough plants. Diplodocids had pencil-shaped teeth. They could strip branches bare in seconds by raking leaves through their teeth.

What were meat-eaters' teeth and claws like?

Meat-eaters such as Allosaurus had long, curved, dagger-like teeth to kill and tear at prey. They had powerful jaws in their large heads and strong claws to grip their victims. Allosaurus could eat you up in two gulps!

 Is it true?
Some dinosaurs ate stones.

Yes. Plant-eaters swallowed stones called gastroliths, to help grind down tough plant food inside their stomachs. Gastroliths were up to four inches across.

Allosaurus

Amazing!
Carcharodontosaurus had a huge skull 5 feet across, with jaws full of teeth like a shark's. And yet some dinosaurs had no teeth at all! Gallimimus fed mainly on insects and tiny creatures it could swallow whole.

Were huge plant-eaters ever attacked?

The sheer size of many of these gentle giants must have put off many predators. Some like Apatosaurus had long claws to defend themselves in case they were attacked. They would rear up on their back legs and slash out at their enemies.

Heterodontosaurus

Amazing! Plant-eaters like Heterodontosaurus had fangs which they may have used to bite attackers. It was a small but strong dinosaur, well able to defend itself against meat-eaters.

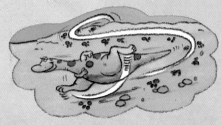

Is it true?
Scientists can tell how quickly dinosaurs could travel.

Yes. By looking at their skeletons and measuring the distance between fossilized footprints, scientists can measure how quickly or slowly a dinosaur moved.

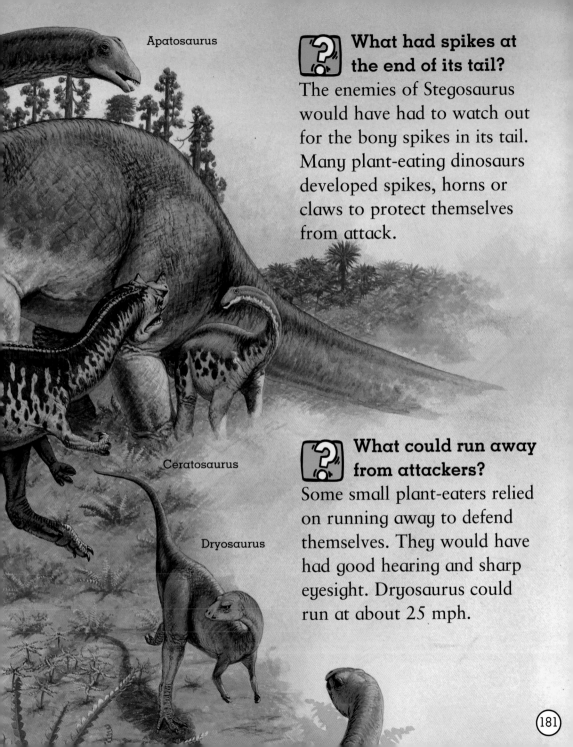

Apatosaurus

What had spikes at the end of its tail?

The enemies of Stegosaurus would have had to watch out for the bony spikes in its tail. Many plant-eating dinosaurs developed spikes, horns or claws to protect themselves from attack.

Ceratosaurus

Dryosaurus

What could run away from attackers?

Some small plant-eaters relied on running away to defend themselves. They would have had good hearing and sharp eyesight. Dryosaurus could run at about 25 mph.

Which dinosaurs used trumpets?

Many 'duck-billed' dinosaurs, like Parasaurolophus, had strange crests on their heads. The male's crest was much larger than the female's. It was hollow and connected to the nostrils. Perhaps these dinosaurs used their crests like trumpets, making sounds to show off to their mates or to threaten rival males.

Parasaurolophus

Is it true?
Scientists were the first people to discover dinosaur tracks.

No. Native Americans were using designs which included dinosaur footprints, long before dinosaur tracks were discovered by scientists.

Pachycephalosaurus

Allosaurus

Diplodocus

What used its tail as a whip?
Diplodocus was a huge, plant-eating dinosaur with an enormously long neck and tail. It could measure 88 feet from nose to tail. When it was attacked, it used its tail like a whip, lashing it from side to side.

What used to fight with its head?
Male dinosaurs probably fought for territory and mates, like animals do today. Pachycephalosaurus had a skull with a dome of thick bone, like a crash helmet. This was probably to protect its brain during head-butting fights with rivals.

Did dinosaurs lay eggs?

Yes. Dinosaurs laid eggs, just as reptiles and birds do today. Scientists have found fossil eggs all over the world. Most are empty, but some eggs have been found with the fossil bones of baby dinosaurs inside.

Centrosaurus

Did dinosaurs protect their young?

Horned dinosaurs like Centrosaurus lived in large family groups, like elephants. When threatened, the adults probably surrounded the young, making a frightening wall of horns.

Maiasaura

Amazing! Oviraptor was thought to live on stolen eggs, because its skeleton was found on the eggs of another dinosaur. But a baby Oviraptor has now been found inside one of the eggs. So scientists can't decide if it's a thief or not!

Is it true?
Dinosaur eggs were huge.

No. Dinosaur eggs were only about 5 inches long. If they were bigger, the shell would have been too thick for the young to break through.

Which reptile made nests?

Maiasaura, 'good mother reptile', made nests in groups. Each parent would dig a hollow in the sand, the female would lay up to 25 eggs, then the eggs were covered with plants to keep them warm.

 Amazing! The largest lizards ever were Mosasaurs, huge reptiles that swam in the sea. They were real sea monsters – 32 feet long with huge mouths, and they looked like dragons! They probably ate anything they could catch.

Were there dinosaurs in the sea?

No. All dinosaurs lived on land, but there was a variety of strange reptiles that swam in the seas in dinosaur times. Ichthyosaurs were strong swimming reptiles that looked like dolphins and could breathe air. They probably hunted in packs, feeding on fish and squid.

Ammonite

Ichthyosaurs

Is it true?
The Loch Ness Monster exists.

Who knows? People who believe that there really is a monster in Loch Ness think it may well be a Plesiosaur. What do you think?

What was all neck?

Plesiosaurs were also swimming reptiles. They had four paddle-like limbs and a tail. Elasmosaurus was a long-necked plesiosaur. Its tiny head sat on an amazingly long neck that was half its total length of 42 feet.

Elasmosaurus

Liopleurodon

What had a huge head?

Liopleurodon was one of the short-necked plesiosaurs. But its head was three feet long! It probably fed on shellfish and turtles, crunching them up with dagger-like teeth that were four inches long.

Why did the dinosaurs disappear?

Some scientists think it was because a large meteorite hit Earth, or because huge volcanoes erupted and the climate changed. Movement of land and seas meant there were also fewer places for dinosaurs to live. It could be all of these reasons.

 Amazing! A huge crater 111 miles across has been found on the seabed near Mexico. It was formed 65 million years ago. Could this be from a meteorite that wiped out the dinosaurs?

Why would a meteorite wipe out the dinosaurs?

When the meteorite hit the surface of the Earth, there would have been a huge explosion. Dust would fill the air, blocking out the Sun's light for several months. Without the Sun vegetation would die, the plant-eaters would die, and finally the large meat-eaters would starve.

Zalambdalestes

Is it true?
People may have caused dinosaurs to become extinct.

No. People and dinosaurs have never lived at the same time. There is a 60 million year gap between the last dinosaurs and the first human beings. So don't believe all the films that you see!

Did all the animals disappear?

No, although many other species died out along with the dinosaurs. These included Pterosaurs and marine reptiles such as Plesiosaurs. Most bigger animals became extinct. But smaller animals survived, and these creatures evolved in a world without the dinosaur.

189

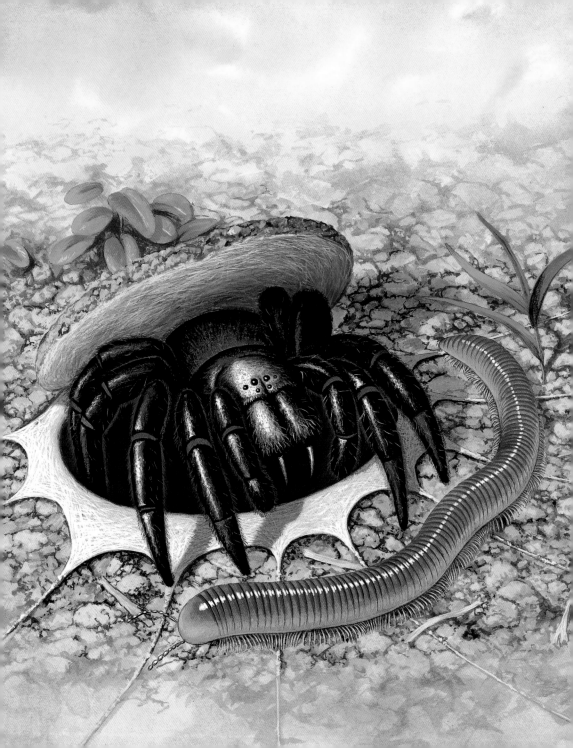

CHAPTER TEN
SPIDERS
AND OTHER CREEPY-CRAWLIES

192 Are spiders insects?

193 What makes an insect an insect?

193 What is a minibeast?

194 Do spiders have teeth?

194 Why do spiders spin webs?

195 What can see with its tail?

196 What is the difference between a centipede and a millipede?

196 What travels on one big foot?

197 How do worms move?

198 What is the difference between a moth and a butterfly?

198 Which butterfly can fly thousands of miles?

199 How do caterpillars become butterflies?

200 When is a plant not a plant?

200 What frightens off enemies with its 'eyes'?

201 What pretends to be dead?

202 What uses a trapdoor to catch its prey?

202 What catches its victims with its lip?

203 What creeps up on its prey?

204 Who makes a good mum?

204 What sits on its eggs until they hatch?

205 How do baby scorpions travel?

206 What lives in a tower block?

207 What makes its nest in a tree?

207 What makes a paper nest?

208 What helps around the house?

209 Who has been sleeping in my bed?

209 Who has been in the cookie jar?

Are spiders insects?

No. Spiders belong to a group called arachnids, which also includes scorpions, mites and ticks. Spiders all have eight legs, one pair more than insects. They have two body parts – a head and an abdomen – and most have eight simple eyes.

Wolf spider

Is it true?

Spiders and insects have bones.

No. Instead they all have a hard casing on the outside called an exoskeleton. This protects their soft insides like a suit of armor and gives them their shape. They have to replace this casing with a new one in order to grow.

Amazing! There are creepy-crawlies living just about everywhere in the world, under water, in caves, down deep holes and even on the tops of mountains. Most of the animals in the world are insects. They make up 85% of all known animal species and there are probably millions more waiting to be discovered!

Head

Thorax

Abdomen

 What makes an insect an insect?

Although they may look different from one another, every adult insect has six legs and three parts to its body. The head is at the front, the thorax in the middle and the abdomen at the back. Many insects have wings for flying and long feelers or antennae.

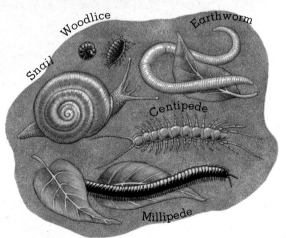

Snail

Woodlice

Earthworm

Centipede

Millipede

What is a minibeast?

Creepy-crawlies can also be called minibeasts. You will find other kinds of minibeasts in this book which are related to spiders and insects, such as woodlice, slugs, snails, worms, centipedes and millipedes.

Do spiders have teeth?

No, but they have fangs for stabbing prey and injecting it with poison and special juices. The victims turn to liquid inside so that the spider can then suck them up like soup!

Indian ornamental tarantula

 Why do spiders spin webs?

Sticky webs can be a home and a trap to catch flying insects. But not all spiders make webs, and not all webs are the same. The ogre-eyed spider makes a web like a net. It hangs down holding the web, waiting to throw it over its prey.

What can see with its tail?

As well as a sting, some scorpions also have light-sensitive cells in their tails. These cells let them know whether it's day or night, even when their heads are underground. Scorpions hunt at night and spend the day hidden in their burrows.

Emperor scorpion

Amazing! The water spider makes its home under the surface of the water. It spins a web like a balloon which it fills with air bubbles. It waits inside until it spots its prey, and then darts out to seize it.

Water spider

Is it true?
Some spiders eat their webs.

Yes. Orb web spiders eat the old web before they spin a new one. A web may take an hour to spin. The silk is as strong as steel of the same thickness.

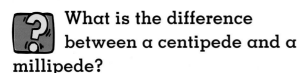

What is the difference between a centipede and a millipede?

Centipedes and millipedes have long, bendy bodies made up of segments. A millipede has two pairs of legs on each segment, but centipedes have only one pair on each segment. Millipedes are plant-eaters. Centipedes are meat-eaters, hunting at night for tiny creatures which they attack with powerful poisonous jaws.

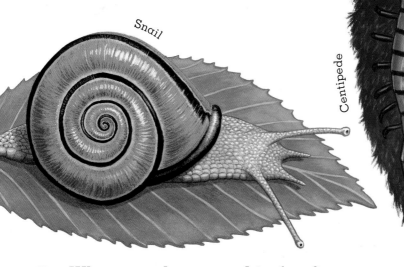

Snail

Centipede

What travels on one big foot?

Snails and slugs glide slowly along on one long muscular foot, leaving a trail of slime behind them. They prefer damp, dark places and are most active at night.

Is it true?
It's a bad thing to have worms in your yard.

No. Gardeners like worms. Earthworms feed on dead plants and soil. As they move through the earth they help mix the soil, which is good. Their burrows put air in the soil and help water to drain away.

How do worms move?

Earthworms live in burrows in the ground. They have no legs, no feet and no skeleton. But their long soft bodies are perfectly shaped to move easily through the earth. They move by stretching and contracting their muscles.

Earthworms

Millipede

Amazing! There are some giant creepy-crawlies. Giant worms in Australia can reach over six feet in length. Some centipedes and millipedes can reach a foot in length. And the largest land snail, the giant African land snail, is a monster compared with the common snail!

197

Croesus moth

Heliconid butterfly

 What is the difference between a moth and a butterfly?
Butterflies are often brightly colored. They fly during the day and their antennae have rounded ends. Moths have feathery antennae, and fly at night.

 Which butterfly can fly thousands of miles?
The American monarch butterfly lives in the United States and Canada. When autumn approaches, thousands travel south to Florida, California and Mexico – a journey of over 1,800 miles.

Peacock butterfly

 Is it true?
Butterflies and moths have scales.

Yes. Butterflies and moths have four wings covered with tiny overlapping scales which shimmer in the light. These scales give them their bold patterns and beautiful colors.

Amazing! Before laying eggs, butterflies test food plants with their antennae and tongues to check that the leaves are suitable for their caterpillars. But some also stamp on the leaves, because butterflies, flies and honeybees have taste organs in their feet!

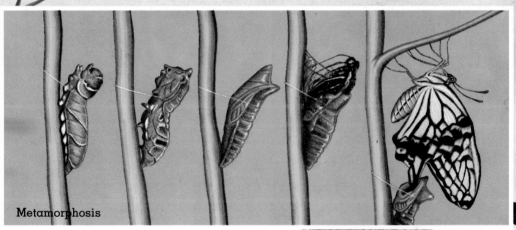

Metamorphosis

 How do caterpillars become butterflies?

When a caterpillar is fully grown, it turns into a pupa. Inside the pupa case the caterpillar's body breaks down and gradually becomes a butterfly. This change is called metamorphosis.

Tortoiseshell butterfly

When is a plant not a plant?

When it's a stick or leaf insect! Stick and leaf insects are the same color and shape as the twigs and leaves on which they feed. During the day they sit very still. Predators leave them alone because they don't realize that they are insects.

Leaf insect

Eyed hawkmoth

What frightens off enemies with its 'eyes'?

The eyed hawkmoth raises its front wings to show bold markings which look like large eyes. This fools enemies into thinking the moth is a much bigger animal than it really is.

Stick insect

 Amazing! Beetles and woodlice have an armor covering so tough that it is difficult to crush. This protects them from their enemies. Some woodlice and millipedes roll into a ball like a hedgehog when they are threatened.

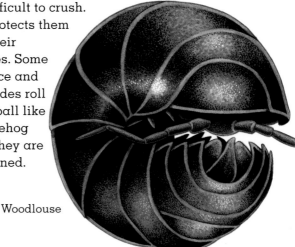

Woodlouse

 What pretends to be dead?

Click beetles lie on their backs as if they were dead to fool their enemies. Then they suddenly spring up in the air, twist and land on their feet, and run away!

 Is it true?
Some spiders can change color.

Yes. Crab spiders can change color to match the flowers they hide in. Lots of insects use camouflage to hide from their enemies. Invisible against the petals, the crab spider can pounce on unsuspecting bees, flies and butterflies as they visit the flower.

What uses a trapdoor to catch its prey?

The trapdoor spider builds an underground burrow, lined with silk and covered with a hinged lid. It lifts up the lid just a little, peeps out and waits. When prey approaches, it flips open the trapdoor, leaps out and attacks.

Trapdoor spider

Young dragonfly

What catches its victims with its lip?

Young dragonflies live in ponds and streams. They catch tadpoles and small fish using a special lower lip, which shoots out to stab and hold prey.

Is it true?

Wasps will not attack spiders.

No. The sting of the large spider wasp can paralyze a spider three times its size. The wasp then lays an egg on the spider. When the larva hatches it eats the spider alive.

Amazing! Spider webs come in many shapes and sizes. The purse web spider spins a long, tube-shaped web. The spider waits inside the web until an unsuspecting insect lands on the outside of the web. Then it bites through the silk and catches its prey.

Millipede

 What creeps up on its prey?

The jumping spider stalks its prey like a cat, before suddenly pouncing. Even with eight eyes, most spiders are short-sighted, and rely on hairs on their legs to sense vibrations. But jumping spiders have excellent eyesight.

Jumping spider

Who makes a good mum?

A female earwig looks after its eggs and young for several months. It keeps the eggs clean and warm, and feeds the young with food from its own stomach.

What sits on its eggs until they hatch?

Some shield bugs protect their eggs by sitting on them. This keeps them safe from hungry predators. After hatching, they look after their young until they can move about.

Shield bug

Amazing! Many bees and wasps live alone. The potter wasp makes a small vase-shaped nest out of clay and saliva. It lays just one egg in it. It then stocks the nest with food for the larva, seals it up and flies off to make another vase.

Potter wasp

Scorpion and young

 How do baby scorpions travel?
Unlike spiders, insects and other creepy-crawlies, scorpions give birth to live young. Some of them are cared for by the mother who carries the whole brood on her back. If one of the young falls off, she places her pincers on the ground so that it can climb back up again.

 Is it true?
A queen bee lays up to 3,500 eggs a day.

Yes. Most creepy-crawlies produce large numbers of eggs. This makes sure that at least some survive to adulthood without getting eaten.

Termite mound

 What lives in a tower block?
Termites build air-conditioned
mounds that can be twenty feet tall. These
nests contain a maze of tunnels and can be
home to millions of termites. Each colony
has a king, a queen and soldiers to guard it.
In countries with a very wet climate, some
termites build mounds with umbrella-
shaped tops.

 Is it true?
An ant's nest is full
of different rooms.

Yes. The nest is made up of
many separate chambers,
connected by a maze of
tunnels. Some rooms are
nurseries for the eggs and
young, others are food
cupboards and some
are trash cans.

Queen termite

What makes a nest in a tree?

Weaver ants make nests by pulling leaves together on a branch. They stick the leaf edges together using sticky silk which they gently squeeze from the ant larvae.

Weaver ants

Paper wasp

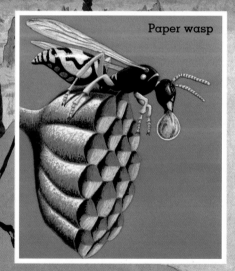

 ## What makes a paper nest?

Paper wasps build nests out of thin sheets of paper. They make the paper themselves by scraping wood from dead trees with their jaws and mixing it with saliva.

Amazing! Like ants and termites, honeybees live with thousands of others in colonies. They work together to find food, care for the young and protect the nest. The nest is made from waxy material which they shape into honeycomb. Honeybee nests are very strong and can last for 50 years.

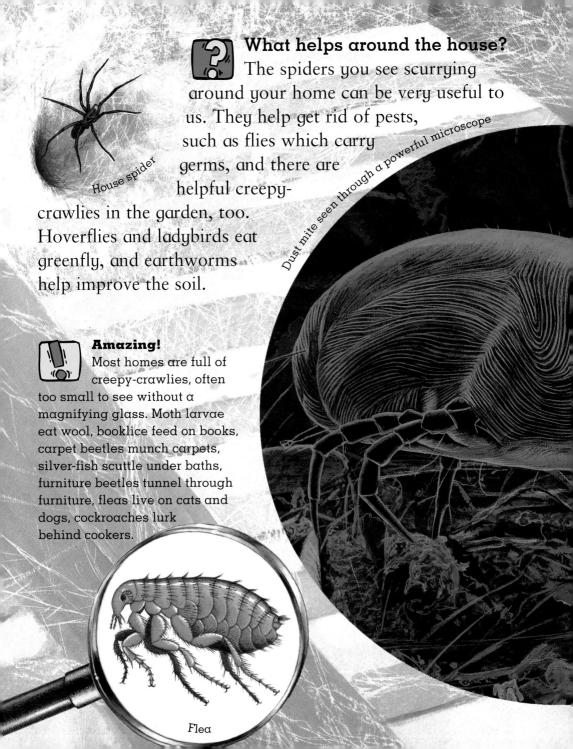

What helps around the house?

The spiders you see scurrying around your home can be very useful to us. They help get rid of pests, such as flies which carry germs, and there are helpful creepy-crawlies in the garden, too. Hoverflies and ladybirds eat greenfly, and earthworms help improve the soil.

House spider

Dust mite seen through a powerful microscope

Amazing!

Most homes are full of creepy-crawlies, often too small to see without a magnifying glass. Moth larvae eat wool, booklice feed on books, carpet beetles munch carpets, silver-fish scuttle under baths, furniture beetles tunnel through furniture, fleas live on cats and dogs, cockroaches lurk behind cookers.

Flea

Who has been sleeping in my bed?

Dust mites are smaller than a period. They live all over the house, but they particularly like beds. Bed bugs are now quite rare, but in some countries they feed on sleeping people.

 Is it true?
Spiders get into the bathtub by climbing up the drainpipe and through the plug hole.

No. It's more likely that they fall down the bathtub's slippery sides, while roaming around our houses looking for a mate.

 ## Who has been in the cookie jar?

Many creepy-crawlies like to live around food. Cheese mites lay their eggs on cheese. Spider beetles eat spices and sauce mixes. An old bag of flour may contain mites, caterpillars and beetles. Guess what the cookie beetle prefers? Hard dry ones luckily, not stickie cookies.

CHAPTER ELEVEN
SNAKES
AND OTHER REPTILES

212 What are reptiles?

213 Which is the shortest snake?

213 Which is the biggest reptile?

214 Why do snakes shed their skin?

215 Which reptile has armor plating?

215 Which snake uses a rattle?

216 Which is the most poisonous land snake?

216 Which snake spits poison?

217 Which snake has the longest fangs?

218 What was the largest snake snack ever eaten?

218 Which snake squeezes its prey to death?

219 Why do snakes have elastic jaws?

220 Which snake pretends to be poisonous?

221 Which snake looks like sand?

221 Where do leaf-tailed geckos hide?

222 Who walks upside down?

222 Which lizard walks on water?

223 Which lizard runs the fastest?

224 Which snakes can fly?

224 Can snakes climb trees?

225 How do snakes slither across loose sand?

226 How well can snakes hear?

227 How do snakes smell with their tongues?

227 Which reptile can look in two ways at once?

228 Which is the longest snake?

229 Which is the biggest lizard?

229 Which reptile lives the longest?

230 Which is the smallest lizard?

230 Which is the largest turtle?

231 Which is the smallest crocodile?

Snake

What are reptiles?

Reptiles are a group of animals which includes snakes, lizards, turtles, tortoises, alligators and crocodiles. They are all vertebrates (they have bones and skeletons inside their bodies), they breathe air and most of them live on land. Their skins are scaly to stop their bodies drying out.

Lizard

Amazing! Lizards love sunbathing. All reptiles are cold-blooded. They can't control their own body temperature but rely on the weather instead. Cold lizards are sluggish and slow. So they warm up in the sun, then scurry off hunting.

Turtle

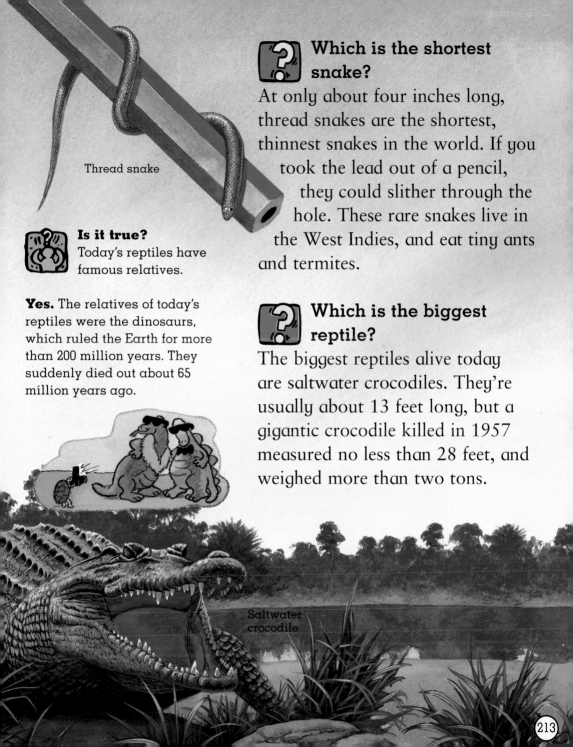

Thread snake

Which is the shortest snake?

At only about four inches long, thread snakes are the shortest, thinnest snakes in the world. If you took the lead out of a pencil, they could slither through the hole. These rare snakes live in the West Indies, and eat tiny ants and termites.

Is it true?
Today's reptiles have famous relatives.

Yes. The relatives of today's reptiles were the dinosaurs, which ruled the Earth for more than 200 million years. They suddenly died out about 65 million years ago.

Which is the biggest reptile?

The biggest reptiles alive today are saltwater crocodiles. They're usually about 13 feet long, but a gigantic crocodile killed in 1957 measured no less than 28 feet, and weighed more than two tons.

Saltwater crocodile

Why do snakes shed their skin?

As a snake grows, its scaly skin gets too small. So the snake grows a new skin underneath, then slithers out of the old one, starting from the head and working down to the tail. A snake sheds its skin in one piece, several times a year.

Reticulated python

Is it true?
You can tell a tortoise's age from its shell.

Yes. A tortoise's shell is made of bone, covered in tough, horny plates. The shell protects the tortoise's body. But that's not all it's good for. Each year, the plates grow a new ring. Count these up, and you can use them to estimate the tortoise's age.

Which reptile has armor plating?

Alligators and crocodiles are covered in tough, horny scales, strengthened with bone. This waterproof armor stops their bodies drying out in the sun, and protects them from enemies.

Amazing! Geckos have see-through eyelids. These are clear flaps of skin which protect their eyes from dust and dirt. A gecko can't blink to clean its eyelids. So it sticks out its tongue and licks them clean.

Which snake uses a rattle?

The rattle at the tip of a rattlesnake's tail is made of hollow scales, loosely linked together. If an enemy gets too close, the rattlesnake shakes its rattle, which makes a loud, angry buzzing sound to scare the attacker away. If this doesn't work, the rattlesnake coils itself up, then strikes with its poisonous fangs.

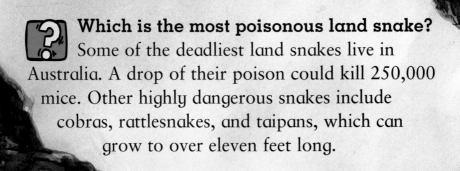

Which is the most poisonous land snake?
Some of the deadliest land snakes live in Australia. A drop of their poison could kill 250,000 mice. Other highly dangerous snakes include cobras, rattlesnakes, and taipans, which can grow to over eleven feet long.

Which snake spits poison?
One type of cobra spits poison in its enemies' faces, blinding the victim! Spitting cobras have very good aims. They can hit a target more than six feet away.

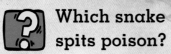

Spitting cobra

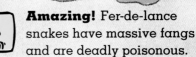

Amazing! Fer-de-lance snakes have massive fangs and are deadly poisonous. They prey on rats and mice. Explorers claimed that local hunters in South America put these lethal snakes in tubes and fired them at their enemies.

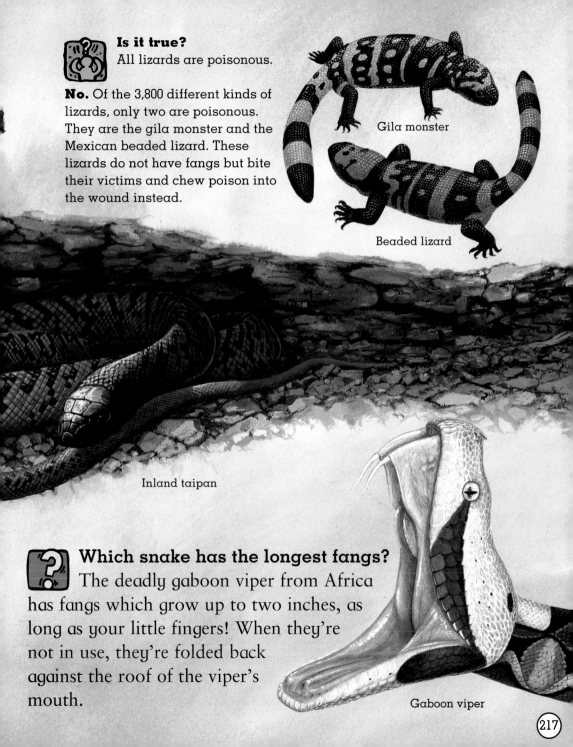

Is it true?

All lizards are poisonous.

No. Of the 3,800 different kinds of lizards, only two are poisonous. They are the gila monster and the Mexican beaded lizard. These lizards do not have fangs but bite their victims and chew poison into the wound instead.

Gila monster

Beaded lizard

Inland taipan

Which snake has the longest fangs?

The deadly gaboon viper from Africa has fangs which grow up to two inches, as long as your little fingers! When they're not in use, they're folded back against the roof of the viper's mouth.

Gaboon viper

What was the largest snake snack ever eaten?

The largest snack ever eaten by a snake was an impala antelope. It was devoured by an African rock python. The snake didn't chew its enormous meal into pieces. It swallowed the impala whole!

Rock python

Impala

Which snake squeezes its prey to death?

A boa constrictor holds its prey in its teeth, then wraps its coils tightly around it. The snake does not crush its victim to death but squeezes it until it suffocates.

Is it true?

A snake can go for more than three years without food.

Yes. It can take a snake weeks to digest a large meal. So they don't need to eat very often. A pit viper once survived without food for three years, three months - a world record.

Why do snakes have elastic jaws?

A snake has sharp, backward-pointing teeth. Its teeth are good at holding food but can't bite it into chunks. Instead, snakes swallow their prey whole. Snakes have amazingly stretchy jaws, with elastic-like hinges between their jawbones. This means they can open their mouths very wide, to swallow food larger than the size of their heads, such as eggs.

Amazing! There are many scary stories of snakes swallowing people. But only a few of them are true. In 1979, a young boy in South Africa was seized by a 14 foot long African rock python. His friends ran off to get help. When they came back about 20 minutes later, the snake had swallowed the boy whole.

219

Which snake pretends to be poisonous?

The milk snake lives in the rainforests of Central America. It's shy, secretive and harmless, but its bright bands of red, yellow and black make it look like the deadly coral snake. Its enemies think the milk snake is equally poisonous, and so leave it well alone.

Vine snake

Milk snake

Coral snake

Is it true?
Some snakes mimic vines.

Yes. The African vine snake hangs down from tree branches, looking just like a harmless vine. There's a nasty suprise for any bird that perches on it. It suddenly snatches the bird and swallows it down.

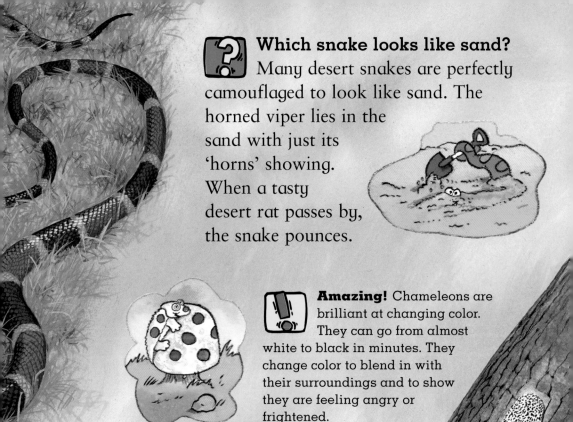

Which snake looks like sand?

Many desert snakes are perfectly camouflaged to look like sand. The horned viper lies in the sand with just its 'horns' showing. When a tasty desert rat passes by, the snake pounces.

Amazing! Chameleons are brilliant at changing color. They can go from almost white to black in minutes. They change color to blend in with their surroundings and to show they are feeling angry or frightened.

Where do leaf-tailed geckos hide?

Pressed upside down against a tree trunk, the leaf-tailed gecko is almost impossible to see. Its body and tail are dappled brown and green to look exactly like the bark of the tree. The ragged fringe of scales around its body and legs hides its outline. It lives on the island of Madagascar.

Leaf-tailed gecko

221

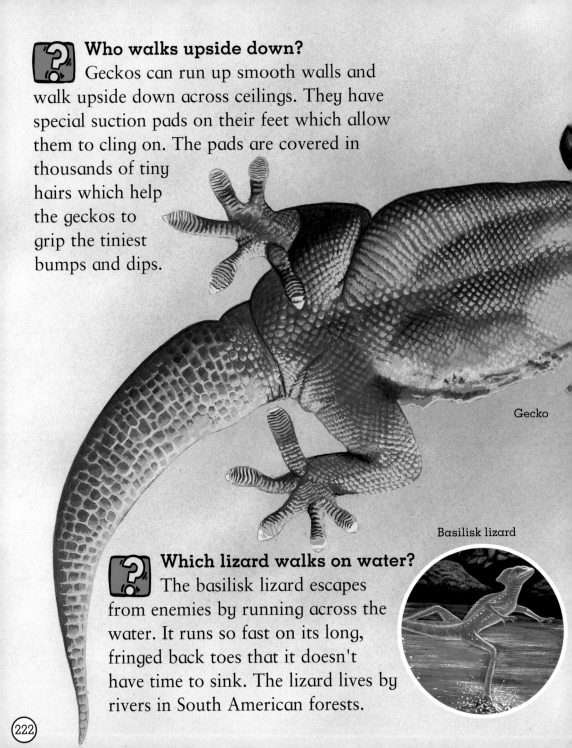

Who walks upside down?

Geckos can run up smooth walls and walk upside down across ceilings. They have special suction pads on their feet which allow them to cling on. The pads are covered in thousands of tiny hairs which help the geckos to grip the tiniest bumps and dips.

Gecko

Basilisk lizard

Which lizard walks on water?

The basilisk lizard escapes from enemies by running across the water. It runs so fast on its long, fringed back toes that it doesn't have time to sink. The lizard lives by rivers in South American forests.

Amazing! Tortoises are real slow-coaches. Their heavy shells weigh them down so much that they move about very slowly, or not at all. Most tortoises lumber along at speeds of less than 0.3 mph, even when they're hungry.

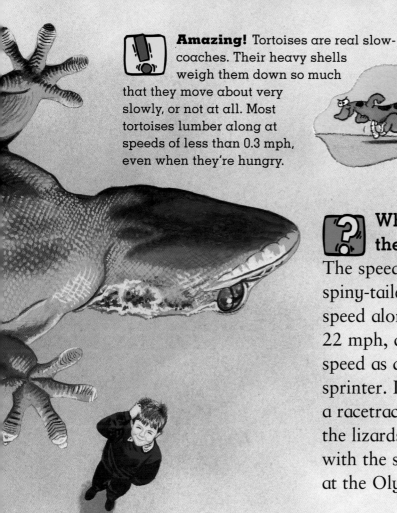

Which lizard runs the fastest?

The speediest lizard is the spiny-tailed iguana. It can speed along at almost 22 mph, about the same speed as a champion sprinter. In an experiment, a racetrack was set up and the lizards were timed with the same devices used at the Olympic Games.

Is it true?
Dragons can fly.

Yes. Flying dragons are small lizards. To travel through the trees, they take to the air. They glide from branch to branch on special 'wings'. These are flaps of skin stretched over very long ribs which stick out from the sides of their body.

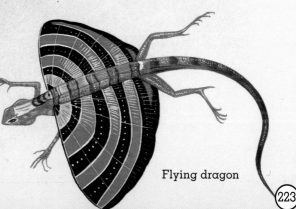

Flying dragon

223

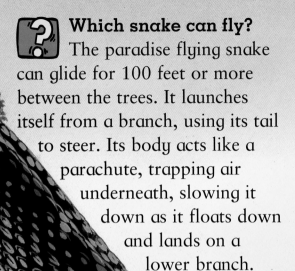

Which snake can fly?

The paradise flying snake can glide for 100 feet or more between the trees. It launches itself from a branch, using its tail to steer. Its body acts like a parachute, trapping air underneath, slowing it down as it floats down and lands on a lower branch.

Flying snake

Amazing! The fastest land snake is the deadly black mamba. There are tales of them overtaking galloping horses. This isn't true but these speedy snakes can race along at about 12 mph.

Black mamba

Can snakes climb trees?

Many snakes slither through the trees, after birds and insects to eat. They are excellent climbers, with rough scales on the underside of their bodies to help them grip slippery branches.

How do snakes slither across loose sand?

Sidewinders have an unusual way of slithering across loose, shifting sand. The sand makes it difficult to get a firm grip. So they flip their bodies sideways in a series of large loops. It leaves a tell-tale set of lines behind in the sand, like the tracks of a bulldozer.

Sidewinder

Is it true?
Snakes once had legs.

Yes. The ancestors of snakes were lizard-like creatures with two pairs of legs. Snakes today do not have legs. Their skeletons are made of a skull, a long backbone and many pairs of ribs. This gives snakes a long, thin shape for slithering across the ground.

Is it true?
Some geckos
bark like dogs.

Yes. The barking gecko
and the tokay gecko
both bark like dogs.
They use their loud
voices to attract mates
or defend their territory.

How well can snakes hear?
Snakes can't hear at all. They
have no outer ears for detecting sounds.
Instead, they pick up vibrations in the
ground through their bodies. Snake
charmers make it look as if a snake is
dancing to the sound of music. But
the snake is actually following the
movement of the snake charmer's
pipe with its eyes, ready to attack.

Spectacled
cobra

Amazing! Crocodiles and
alligators are very noisy.
They cough, hiss and bellow
to attract mates and keep in touch
with their group. The American
alligator roars like a lion. It can be
heard about 500 feet away.

 ## How do snakes smell with their tongues?

Snakes don't smell things through their noses like we do. They pick up smell with their tongues, which they flick in and out. They can recognize different smells with the Jacobson's organ in the roof of the mouth.

Jacobson's organ

 ## Which reptile can look in two ways at once?

Chameleons can move each of their large, bulging eyes on its own. This means they can look in two ways at once. When they're hunting, one eye can look out for tasty insects to eat. The other can watch out for hungry enemies.

Chameleon

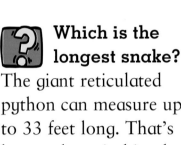

Amazing! The lizard-like tuatara is the only survivor of a group of reptiles that lived in the time of the dinosaurs. By 65 million years ago, the rest of the group had died out. Only the tuatara was left. Tuataras are only found in New Zealand. Their name means 'spiny backed' in the local Maori language.

Which is the longest snake?

The giant reticulated python can measure up to 33 feet long. That's longer than six bicycles standing end to end. No snake could grow longer than 50 feet. It would be too heavy to move.

Reticulated python

Is it true?

Sea snakes are the most poisonous snakes.

Yes. All sea snakes are poisonous. One of the most poisonous of all is the banded sea snake from around Australia. Its venom is many times stronger than the deadliest land snake. Luckily, this snake rarely bites human beings.

Sea snake

Komodo dragon

Which is the biggest lizard?

The Komodo dragon is the world's largest lizard. Males can grow more than nine feet long and weigh more than 330 pounds. These record-breaking reptiles live on a few islands in Indonesia. They are meat-eaters and can swallow deer and pigs whole!

Which reptile lives the longest?

Tortoises live longer than any other animals on land. The oldest tortoise known was a Marion's tortoise from the Seychelles. When it died in 1918, it was thought to be over 150 years old.

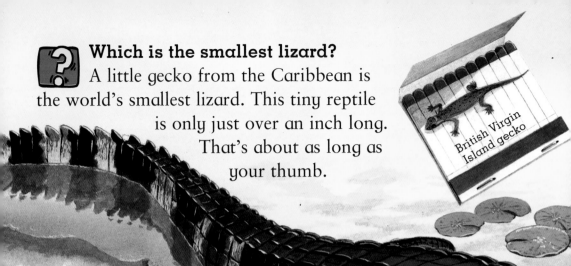

Which is the smallest lizard?

A little gecko from the Caribbean is the world's smallest lizard. This tiny reptile is only just over an inch long. That's about as long as your thumb.

British Virgin Island gecko

Dwarf caiman

Which is the largest turtle?

The leatherback turtle is about the size of a small car. This giant reptile can grow almost ten feet long, from its head to the tip of its tail. It measures nearly ten feet across its front flippers. It can weigh almost a ton.

Leatherback turtle

Is it true?
Most poisonous snakes live in Africa.

No. Eight out of ten of the world's deadliest snakes live in Australia. About 3,000 people are bitten by snakes there every year. Luckily, very few of these snakebites are fatal.

Which is the smallest crocodile?

The smallest crocodile is the dwarf caiman which lives in South America. This mini crocodile only grows about five feet long, about a third of the size of its giant cousin, the massive saltwater crocodile.

Amazing! At almost a quarter of a ton, the anaconda from South America is the world's bulkiest snake. This heavyweight snake lies in sluggish rivers or streams, waiting for prey to come down to drink. Then it grabs its victim in its mouth and squeezes it to death.

CHAPTER TWELVE
SHARKS
AND OTHER DANGEROUS FISH

What are sharks?

Sharks are meat-eating sea fish. Most have sleek bodies and rows of sharp teeth. There are about 375 types, of different shapes and sizes, living in different parts of the world. The dwarf shark is only four inches long, while the whale shark, the biggest of all fish, is 50 feet.

Hammerhead shark

How old are sharks?

Fossils show that sharks appeared more than 350 million years ago, long before the dinosaurs. Megalodon was a huge shark which hunted large prey and probably ate shellfish too. Its teeth were about three inches long.

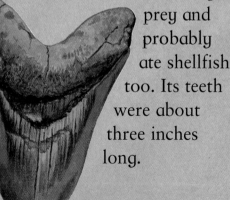

Megalodon tooth

Amazing! Sharks become sluggish in cool water, and so most prefer to live in warm seas. But the huge Greenland shark, twenty feet long, enjoys icy water. It lives in the North Atlantic, hunting for fish and seals beneath the pack ice.

Whale shark

Manta ray

Basking shark

Is it true?
All sharks are dangerous.

No. In the order of dangerous sharks, the great white is most feared by people. But most sharks are harmless to us, and will only attack if they are disturbed. Other dangerous sharks include the tiger shark, mako, bronze and black-tipped whalers, and hammerhead.

Are sharks different from other fish?

Sharks, and their relatives the skates and rays, have skeletons made of rubbery cartilage. Other fish have skeletons made of bone. A shark's gill slits are not covered like other fish, but are in a row behind its head.

 Is it true?
Sharks never have
a break.

No. Sharks living near the
surface must swim all their
lives to avoid sinking. But
others like the nurse shark
spend most of their time
motionless on the seabed.
Nurse sharks can pump
water over their gills
and so they don't
need to keep
moving.

How fast can a shark swim?
Sharks such as the mako shark
are perfect swimming machines,
capable of speeds of up to
45 mph. Their sleek
shape means they can
move quickly through
the water and turn
at speed.

Grey reef shark

 **Why are sharks darker
on top?**
Sharks that swim near the
surface are dark on top and
paler on their undersides. This
means they are difficult to see
from above or below as they
hunt for prey.

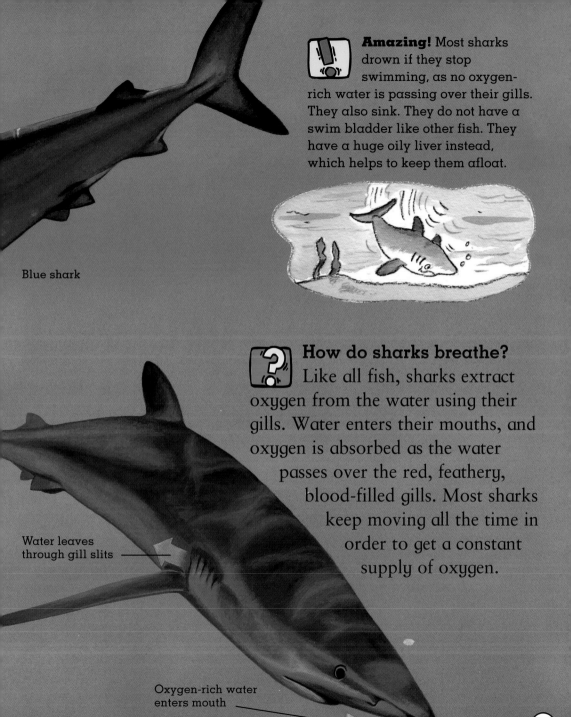

Amazing! Most sharks drown if they stop swimming, as no oxygen-rich water is passing over their gills. They also sink. They do not have a swim bladder like other fish. They have a huge oily liver instead, which helps to keep them afloat.

Blue shark

How do sharks breathe?
Like all fish, sharks extract oxygen from the water using their gills. Water enters their mouths, and oxygen is absorbed as the water passes over the red, feathery, blood-filled gills. Most sharks keep moving all the time in order to get a constant supply of oxygen.

Water leaves through gill slits

Oxygen-rich water enters mouth

Sand tiger shark

 Do sharks have the same senses as us?

Sharks have the five senses of sight, smell, taste, hearing and touch. They also have one more. Sensitive cells on their snouts allow them to pick up tiny electrical signals from other animals.

Reef sharks

 How do sharks know when an animal is struggling nearby?

Sharks can tell that there are animals in their area, even when there is no blood to smell. A sensitive 'lateral line' along their bodies allows them to feel ripples in the water from any struggling animal or person.

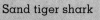
Lateral line

238

Do sharks have good eyesight?
Sight is important in the final moments of a shark's hunt. But sharks depend much more on their sense of smell. Sharks get very excited at the smell of blood. They can smell a drop of blood, diluted millions of times, half a mile away.

Amazing! Most fish have scaly skin, but a shark's tough skin and scales are very different. They are sharp points called denticles which are like teeth. Shark skin was once used for smoothing down wood, instead of sandpaper.

Is it true?
Sharks nudge their food before they take a bite.

Yes. They sometimes nudge an object or animal with their snout before they decide whether to eat it or not! Perhaps they can 'taste' it with special cells in their skin.

Denticles

What is known as the trash can of the sea?

Tiger sharks will eat anything. They are not put off by a crunchy turtle shell, or a stinging jellyfish, or even a poisonous snake. They will happily munch dead animals that have been washed out to sea, old boots, papers, tin cans, plastic bags – and even people!

Tiger shark

Amazing! Sometimes when a shark feeds, others join in. They get excited at the blood and movement around them, and seem to go crazy, biting, twisting and turning wildly in a 'feeding frenzy'.

How many teeth do sharks have?

Sharks are born with jaws full of teeth, neatly arranged in rows. They grow teeth all their lives. When front ones wear out or are lost, they're replaced by new teeth behind.

Sand tiger shark

Is it true?
A shark's teeth last for months.

No. Once a rear tooth has moved to the front row, it may drop out, snap off or be worn away in as little as two weeks.

Do all sharks have the same teeth?

The shape and size depend on a shark's food. For example, the great white has slicing teeth for tearing off chunks of seal or dolphin. The Port Jackson has sharp front teeth to hold shellfish, and blunt back teeth to crush them.

Tiger shark tooth

Mako tooth

Great white shark tooth

 ## What is the biggest fish in the world?

The biggest fish is also one of the most harmless, the whale shark. It measures 50 feet long and weighs about 13 tons. It swims slowly through the sea with its mouth open wide, filtering millions of tiny creatures from the water.

 Is it true?
You could hitch a ride on a whale shark.

Yes. These gentle giants have been known to allow scuba divers to hang on to their fins and ride with them.

Whale shark

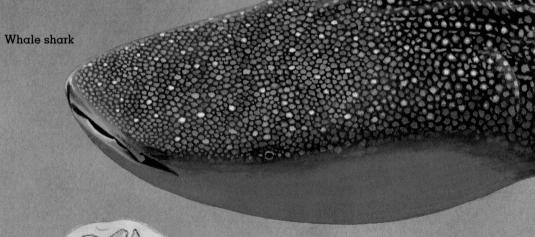

Amazing! Little is known about the megamouth. But we do know that it has luminous organs that give off a glow around its lips. Scientists think this may be to tempt tiny creatures into its mouth.

Basking shark

? **Which shark appears to sunbathe?**
Basking sharks spend much of their time wallowing at the ocean's surface, especially when it's sunny – probably because there's more food there on sunny days, not because they want a suntan!

Megamouth

? **What has a huge mouth?**
The megamouth shark lives in deep, dark seas. Like the whale shark, it swims with its enormous mouth wide open, filtering water for food. It is very rare and only a few have ever been seen.

Which shark has wings?

Angel sharks have very large pectoral fins, like an angel's wings. They spend much of their lives on the ocean floor, waiting for fish or shellfish to come along so they can snap them up.

Is it true?

Angel sharks look like monks.

Yes. Angel sharks are also called monkfish because their heads are the same shape as a monk's hood.

Angel shark

Port Jackson shark

What is a 'pig fish'?

The Port Jackson shark is known as the 'pig fish', or 'bulldog shark'. It has a blunt head and a squashed nose with very large nostrils for finding sea urchins and shellfish.

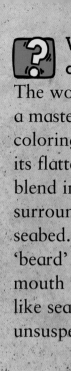

Which shark uses a disguise?

The wobbegong shark is a master of disguise. The coloring and markings of its flattened body help it blend into its surroundings on the seabed. It also has a 'beard' of skin around its mouth which looks just like seaweed to unsuspecting prey.

Amazing! If a swell shark is attacked by a predator, it gulps down as much sea water as it can, and swells up like a balloon. It then jams itself into a crack in a rock where its enemy can't reach it.

Wobbegong

Which mysterious shark has a very long snout?

Goblin sharks were discovered 100 years ago and yet we still know very little about them. They live in deep water, and use their long, sensitive snouts to seek out prey.

Goblin shark

 What has a head like a hammer?

The head of a hammerhead shark is spread out to form a T-shape with its body. Its eyes are on each end of the 'hammer'. As it swims, it swings its head from side to side so it can look around.

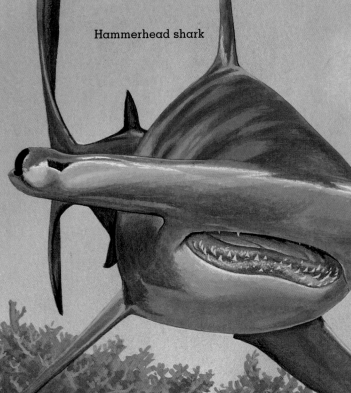
Hammerhead shark

 Is it true?
Cookiecutter sharks can glow.

Yes. These small sharks have light organs on their undersides, which glow, maybe to persuade their prey to come close to them.

 ## What bites chunks out of its prey?

Cookiecutter sharks are often happy with just a bite or two from their prey, which includes whales, seals and dolphins. The wounds they make with their small teeth are oval-shaped, a bit like a cookie.

Seal wounded by cookiecutter

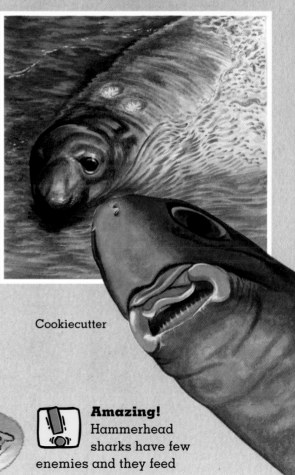

Cookiecutter

Amazing! Hammerhead sharks have few enemies and they feed alone. Yet they sometimes gather together in large 'schools', where hundreds all swim together.

Yes. Sawfish and saw sharks have long sharp snouts studded with teeth, like a saw. They use their snouts to dig in the mud for food and to slash at other fish. The six types of sawfish belong to the same group as rays.

What is called the devilfish?

Manta rays are also known as devilfish, even though they are harmless and feed on plankton. They are the largest of all rays, at 23 feet across. They flap their huge fins like wings, which makes them look as if they're flying slowly and gracefully through the water.

Manta ray

Electric ray

Which fish can shock?

The electric ray has special electric organs just behind its head. It gives off bursts of electricity to defend itself or to stun the fish it feeds on.

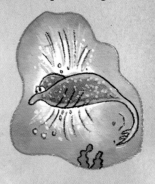

What has a sting on its tail?

Stingrays have poisonous spines on their whip-like tails. Some have one poisonous spine, others have several. They lie on the seabed with only their eyes and tail showing.

Stingray

Shark-proof bag

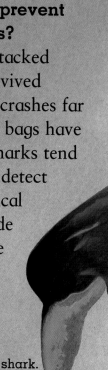

Amazing! In Australia in the 1930s, hundreds of sharks were caught in nets in just a few months. The numbers of many large sharks have gone down sharply all over the world because of hunting.

How can we prevent shark attacks?

Sharks have often attacked people who have survived shipwrecks or plane crashes far out at sea. Inflatable bags have been tested, which sharks tend to avoid. They can't detect moving limbs, electrical signals or blood inside them. Beaches can be protected by nets.

Is it true?
Nothing attacks a shark.

No. Sharks will attack each other. They are also attacked by whales, and even dolphins who will group together to protect their young. But the biggest threat of all comes from people.

Surfer on board

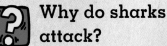

Why do sharks attack?

When a shark attacks, it is often because it mistakes a swimmer or surfer for a seal or other prey. About 100 shark attacks are recorded on people each year. Many of the victims survive.

Seal

Great white shark

Shark cage

Who swims inside a cage?

Scientists studying dangerous sharks, such as the ocean white-tip and bull shark, often protect themselves inside a cage. The shark can bang the cage as much as it likes, but the diver is safe inside.

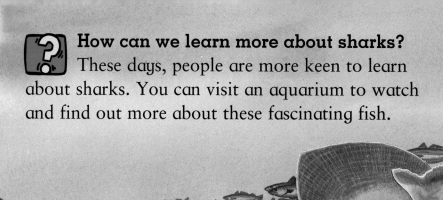

How can we learn more about sharks?

These days, people are more keen to learn about sharks. You can visit an aquarium to watch and find out more about these fascinating fish.

Amazing! Scientists can now tell a lot from some sharks' behavior. By studying a creature's movements and senses, they know when a shark is just being nosy, or when it's about to attack. By learning more, we may kill fewer sharks, and suffer fewer shark attacks.

Why do people kill sharks?

People kill millions of sharks every year, some to protect swimmers, others for food or just for sport. If too many are killed, sharks might disappear altogether.

Fisherman and catch

Which scientists dress like knights of old?

Scientists studying sharks sometimes wear chain-mail suits for protection. They may tag a shark's fins to learn how quickly and far it can travel.

Diver in chain-mail with blue shark

 **Is it true?**
We've discovered all the sharks that exist.

No. Megamouth was first seen in 1976. Scientists think that there might be more sharks waiting to be discovered in the depths of the oceans.

CHAPTER THIRTEEN
BIRDS OF PREY
AND OTHER FEATHERED FRIENDS

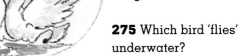

❓ Which are the biggest birds?

Albatross

The African ostrich can grow to over eight feet tall, which is much taller than the average man. The huge wandering albatross has the largest wingspan in the world, at nearly ten feet. Its long, pointed wings make it an excellent glider.

Ostrich

Amazing! There are around 9,000 different kinds of birds, in many colors, shapes and sizes. They live all over world, in steamy jungles, icy regions, by the sea, in towns, and some move from one area to another when they migrate.

256

Which are the smallest birds?

Hummingbirds are the smallest birds in world. The bee hummingbird of Cuba is no bigger than a bumblebee! Hummingbirds can flap their wings at up to 90 beats per second. They get their name from the humming sound their wings make.

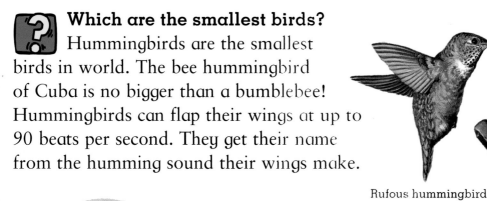

Rufous hummingbird

What are birds?

Birds all have two legs, two wings, a beak, they lay eggs and they are the only animals that have feathers. But not all birds can fly, and not all flying animals are birds.

Is it true?
The first bird dates back to dinosaur times.

Black-faced ant thrush

Yes. Archaeopteryx is the earliest bird-like creature that we know of. It lived 150 million years ago. It had a head like a reptile, sharp teeth, a long tail and feathered wings.

Sparrowhawk

What is a bird of prey?

Birds of prey catch and eat other animals. They are excellent hunters, with strong hooked beaks and sharp claws called talons, which they use to kill and tear at prey.

Why are birds of prey good hunters?

The eyes of a bird of prey are different from other birds' eyes. They're very big, and face forwards so they can judge detail and distance well. A buzzard's eyes are as big as yours!

Buzzard

Amazing! Eagles can catch animals much bigger and heavier than themselves. The harpy eagle which lives in South American jungles is the biggest eagle of all. It has huge feet which it uses for grabbing and crushing monkeys and other animals.

Is it true?
Some birds eat eggs.

Yes. The Egyptian vulture uses stones to break into its favorite food, ostrich eggs. Birds can have very fussy tastes. Bat hawks, for example, only eat bats. Some eagles eat fish, while others prefer snakes.

How do ospreys hunt?
Ospreys fly high above the water looking for fish. When they spot one, they dive and enter the water feet-first to catch it. Their toes have tiny sharp spikes for gripping slippery fish.

Osprey

Why do birds have feathers?

Birds have three different kinds of feathers: down to keep warm; body feathers to cover and protect; and flight feathers. Baby birds have down feathers and can't fly until they've grown all their flight feathers.

Albatross chick

 Is it true?
All flamingos are pink.

No. In the wild, flamingos are generally pink. Color from the food is absorbed and passes to the feathers. But in captivity, their feathers can turn white if they have a change of diet.

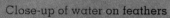
Close-up of water on feathers

 ## How do birds keep clean?

All birds comb, or preen, their feathers with their beaks and claws. Love birds preen each other. Most birds also spread oil on their feathers from a gland above the tail, which keeps them waterproof.

Why are some feathers bright and others dull?

Many woodland birds, such as the tawny frogmouth, have dull feathers so that they can blend in with their background and keep safe. Male birds are often more brightly colored to attract a mate.

Tawny frogmouth and chick

Amazing! Most birds have over 1,000 feathers and some birds have an enormous number. Swans have about 25,000 feathers – more than almost any other bird!

How do birds fly?

Birds need to be light but strong to fly. They flap their wings to take off and fly higher in air. As the wing flaps down, the flight feathers close against the air, which pushes the bird up and forward.

Reed warbler

What has to run to take off?

Swans are too big and heavy to leap into the air. Instead they have to run along the surface of the water, flapping their powerful wings to get enough speed to take off.

Swan

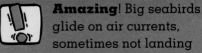

Amazing! Big seabirds glide on air currents, sometimes not landing for weeks. Other birds can stay in the air for months, while swifts can spend years in the air, only landing to nest and mate.

Kestrel

What can fly and yet stay in the same spot?

Kestrels are experts at hovering. They fly into the wind and beat their wings very quickly. This lets them stay in the same position as they search for prey below.

Is it true?
Birds can only fly forwards.

No. Hummingbirds are special. They can fly forwards, sideways, backwards and hover on the spot by flapping their wings very quickly!

Pelican

? Whose beak can hold more than its stomach?

A pelican has a beak with a stretchy pouch which can hold far more fish than its stomach! It scoops fish from the water using its beak like a fishing net.

Amazing! A woodpecker uses its unusual beak to drill for insects, to make holes in dying trees to use as nests, and to hammer on a tree to mark its territory.

Why do birds have beaks?

Birds use their beaks to catch and hold food, to make nests and to preen themselves. They have different beaks because they eat different food. The toucan uses its enormous beak to pull fruits from delicate branches.

Toucan

Is it true?
Birds have teeth?

No. Birds cannot chew, so they grind food up with a gizzard inside their bodies, and sometimes by swallowing small stones too.

Yellow-headed parrot

What climbs with its beak?

Parrots usually live in big noisy groups in tropical forests. They have short, curved powerful beaks for cracking nuts and seeds. Some parrots have beaks so strong that they can even use them to pull themselves up trees.

Why do ducks have webbed feet?

Water birds have skin between their toes. Their feet are like paddles, helping them move easily through the water. They can also walk on mud without sinking in.

African jacana

Redhead duck

 Amazing! Jacanas are water birds that live in tropical places. Their very long toes allow them to step on water plants without sinking. They are sometimes called 'lily-trotters'.

 Is it true?
Birds stand on one leg when they've hurt their foot.

No. When a bird stands on one leg, it is keeping the other foot warm, tucked up under its feathers.

Heron

What has legs like stilts?

Herons and storks have very long legs which look like stilts. They are ideal for standing or wading in shallow water, where the birds use their long beaks to catch fish and frogs.

Budgerigar

Why don't birds fall when they sleep?

Birds have a long tendon attached to each toe. When they rest on branches or another perch, they bend their legs and their toes lock around the perch.

Most birds build nests to hide their eggs and to keep their young warm and safe from enemies. Colonies of weaver birds often build several nests in the same tree.

Black-headed weaver birds

Hummingbird's nest

Amazing! Some nests are huge. An eagle's nest or eyrie is so big that you could lie down in it! Some birds, such as the hummingbird, make tiny nests. The bee hummingbird's nest is the same size as a thimble.

Thrushes

Why do birds sit on their eggs?

Birds sit on their eggs to keep them warm while the baby birds inside grow. If the eggs get cold, the babies inside will die, so birds don't leave their eggs alone for long.

(269)

Is it true?
Nests are birds'
homes where they
sleep at night.

No. Birds only use nests for
laying eggs and raising their
chicks. They rest at night in
hedges, trees or holes.

Do birds' eggs all look the same?
Birds' eggs are often coloured or
patterned for camouflage. The
guillemot's eggs are also an
unusual shape. They are pointed
at one end so that if nudged,
they spin in a circle instead
of rolling off a cliff.

What do newly hatched birds look like?

The young of tree-nesting birds are naked and blind at first. Their parents have to look after them, and they are always hungry! They open their beaks wide and call loudly, which forces the parents to feed them.

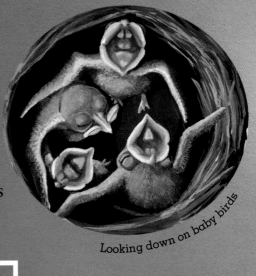

Looking down on baby birds

Grebe with young

 What sits on its mother's back?

Baby grebes can swim soon after they hatch. When they get cold or tired, they sit on their mother's back to warm up and have a rest.

Amazing! The hummingbird lays the world's smallest eggs. Each is only the size of your fingernail. Compared to this, an ostrich egg is huge, and thousands of times heavier.

Which father sits on his eggs until they hatch?

The male ostrich makes eggs with up to twelve different females. The females all lay their eggs in same nest. The male then sits on them himself until they hatch. Many types of male bird, including pigeons, take it in turns with the female to sit on the eggs.

Ostriches and chicks

Is it true?
A duckling could mistake you for its mother.

Yes. A duckling thinks that the first creature it sees after hatching is its mother. If you were around, that would be you!

Which bird calls to find its nest?

When a male gannet has caught fish for his mate and young, he must call out and wait for the female's reply before he can find them amongst all the other gannets.

Gannets

Why do birds sing?

Birds sing most of all during the breeding season. A male bird sings to attract a mate, or to tell other birds to keep away from his territory. Males and females also call to warn other birds that an enemy is near, such as a cat or a human.

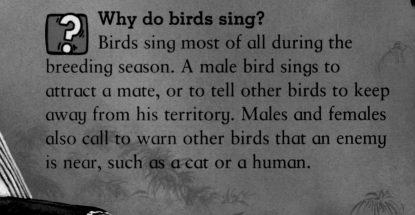

Magpie lark

Which birds copy sounds?

Some birds are natural mimics. This means they can copy sounds, such as the telephone ringing or even human speech. The mynah bird used to be popular as a caged pet because of this talent. Australian lyrebirds can even imitate a chainsaw!

Superb lyrebird

Amazing! The African grey parrot is a real chatterbox. It can learn up to 800 different words, but it doesn't know what they mean!

Is it true? Birds can sing very high notes.

Yes. Many birds can sing notes too high for us to hear! There is a wide range of beautiful birdsong, full of high and low notes.

What was a dodo?

Have you heard the expression 'as dead as a dodo'? Dodos were strange-looking, heavy birds that could not fly. They lived on islands in the Indian Ocean until sailors hunted the very last one. Sadly, they have been extinct since 1800.

Dodo

Kiwi

What has invisible wings?

Kiwis are flightless birds whose wings are so tiny that you cannot see them. They have long whiskers, no tail and a good sense of smell. They hunt at night for worms and insects.

Which bird 'flies' underwater?

Penguins are water birds which cannot fly. They live in the chilly Antarctic. They slide on snow and ice using their bellies as toboggans. But in water they are very graceful, using their wings as flippers as they swim along catching fish.

Is it true?
Penguins argue with their wings.

Yes. Penguins live close together. When they squabble with each other, they flap their wings and jab their beaks to help make their point!

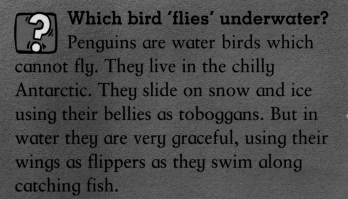

King penguins

Amazing! Ostriches cannot fly, but they can run very quickly indeed. The African ostrich can sprint along at 40 mph! They live in dry grasslands and may have to travel a long way for food.

CHAPTER FOURTEEN
WILD CATS
AND OTHER DANGEROUS PREDATORS

278 What do cats, dogs and bears have in common?

279 What is a Tasmanian devil?

279 Are hyenas dogs?

280 Can any animal outrun a cheetah?

281 How does the cheetah kill its prey?

281 Where do cheetah cubs live?

282 Who's the biggest cat of all?

282 How big is a tiger's paw?

283 How many tigers are there?

284 Which leopard has lost its spots?

284 Who hides in the trees?

285 Who hides a feast in the trees?

286 Do hyenas laugh?

287 Do hyena cubs get on together?

287 Do hyenas hunt?

288 How do dogs hunt?

288 Do dogs use babysitters?

289 What do pups eat?

290 Which is the biggest dog?

291 Do wolves howl at the Moon?

291 Which wolf walks on stilts?

292 Which is the biggest bear?

293 Which cubs drink the creamiest milk?

293 Can bears walk on water?

294 Which bear fishes for its supper?

294 When do bears climb trees?

295 Do all bears eat meat?

What do cats, dogs and bears have in common?

They are all mammals. This means that they are covered with cosy fur and feed their young with mother's milk. Cats, dogs and bears are also all carnivores, which means they eat meat. To do this, they have special sharp, pointy teeth, called canines.

Grizzly bear

Is it true?

Cats, dogs and bears are the only carnivores in the world.

No. Many other mammals, such as hyenas, weasels, raccoons and humans eat meat. So do other animals – birds of prey, some reptiles and sharks in the sea.

Great white shark

Amazing! There were mammals around at the same time as the dinosaurs. Just like dinosaurs, some were carnivorous (meat-eating), such as Zalambdalestes, and some were herbivores (vegetarians).

Tasmanian devil

What is a Tasmanian devil?

The Tasmanian devil lives in Tasmania, an island south of mainland Australia, and belongs to the same mammal family as kangaroos, carrying its babies in a pouch on its tummy. It's small, ferocious, and can defend itself well against other predators.

Are hyenas dogs?

No, though they look quite similar. Hyenas hunt in packs like dogs, but they have four toes per foot, whereas dogs have five on their front paws. Hyenas are not cats either, but are closely related.

Can any animal outrun a cheetah?

Over short distances, the cheetah tops 600 miles per hour, and no animal can beat that. Cheetahs reach such high speeds partly because their dog-like claws work like running shoes and give them a good grip. But the speed king soon runs out of puff. If an impala keeps ahead for more than 550 yards, its life is saved – at least this time!

Cheetah

Impala

Amazing! The average cheetah hunt is over in seconds! A cheetah may spend hours lazing about lying in wait, but it normally runs down its prey within 300 yards. It takes the cat less than 20 seconds to catch its meal!

Cheetah with prey

How does the cheetah kill its prey?

The cheetah lives on the African grasslands. It usually chases animals such as antelopes, gazelles, or even ostriches. When it catches up with its fast-running prey, it fells and kills it by clamping its strong jaws on to its neck.

Is it true?
Cheetahs are spotted all over.

No. The cheetah is mostly spotted, but its tail is striped. And the king cheetah, which is extremely rare, has stripes on its back where the spots have joined up.

Where do cheetah cubs live?

Cheetah mothers don't have a permanent den. Instead, they move their cubs around a couple of times each week. This stops other big cats finding and preying on them.

Cheetah and cub

Is it true?
Tigers don't attack a victim
which looks them in the eye.

Yes. Tigers usually attack from behind.
In Southeast Asia, people sometimes
wear masks that act as fake faces, on
the backs of their heads.

Who's the biggest cat of all?

The Siberian tiger can reach
a record-breaking eleven feet
long – that's about six times
longer than a pet cat. This
tiger is very rare and lives in
the mountains of northern
China and Russia. Its long,
off-white, striped fur keeps
it warm and hidden in the
snow.

Siberian tiger

How big is a tiger's paw?

Huge – almost as big as a
grown-up's head! Even a gentle
swipe of its paw would easily
knock you off your feet.

282

Amazing! The cub of a male tiger and a female lion is called a tigon. Lions and tigers are so closely related that they have been bred together in zoos. Ligers are the cubs of a female tiger and a male lion.

How many tigers are there?

There are five main types of tiger – the Siberian, South Chinese, Sumatran, Indochinese and Indian. The number of tigers has fallen faster than for any other cat. There are fewer than 5,000 in the world today.

Caspian tiger (probably extinct)

Which leopard has lost its spots?

The black panther, which is really a type of leopard! But if you were brave, or foolish, enough to get close to a panther, you'd see faint spots in its fur.

Who hides in the trees?

Lots of spotted cats, including leopards and jaguars, hide in the trees to take a catnap or lie in wait for their prey. The dappled light through the leaves makes everything look spotted, so their coats are the perfect camouflage.

Leopard

Leopard

Amazing! The snow leopard is a champion long-jumper! This rare big cat can clear a 5 foot wide ditch – that's over one and a half times further than the human long-jump record.

Who hides a feast in the trees?

Sometimes leopards kill such big prey, that they can't eat it all in one go. Leopards can drag a whole deer up into the branches of a tree, safe from jackals and hyenas, which can't climb up and steal it!

Jaguar swimming

Is it true?
All cats hate the water.

No. Quite a few types of cat enjoy a swim. Jaguars in the South American rainforests often bathe in the River Amazon. They love to snack on river turtles and sometimes even kill crocodiles!

Do hyenas laugh?

The spotted, or laughing, hyena has two different calls. One sounds like a laugh, but the other sounds more like a wail. This hyena is very daring. It has attacked sleeping people and has even carried off young children!

Amazing! Hyenas work as refuse collectors. Hyenas are scavengers – they will eat just about anything. In some African villages hyenas are sometimes allowed in to clear the trash.

Spotted hyenas

Is it true?
All hyenas have manes.

No. Spotted hyenas don't, but striped hyenas and brown hyenas do. They have scruffy-looking hair sticking up around their head and even down their back.

Do hyena cubs get on together?

Hyena cubs play with each other to practice the skills they'll need as adults, but they don't really get on. Twins fight over food, and sometimes, the weaker twin slowly starves to death.

Hyena cubs

Vultures

Lioness with prey

Do hyenas hunt?

Spotted hyenas do, but other hyenas prefer other animals to do the work for them! Most hyenas feed mainly on carrion, which is a bigger hunter's leftovers. When they do hunt for themselves, hyenas go for wildebeest, zebra, or they steal a goat or cow from the local farmer.

How do dogs hunt?

Many dogs, including African wild dogs, hunt in groups called packs. First they spread out, so they have a good view of the landscape, then they close in on their prey. They keep in contact with barks and body language.

African wild dogs

Warthog

Do dogs use babysitters?

Yes! Jackals in particular live in very close-knit family groups. They share all the jobs. Sometimes a young female jackal is picked to stay at home looking after the cubs while all the other mothers go out hunting.

Yes. But the African wild
dog is the one exception.
This fierce hunter is missing
a toe on each front foot.

African wild dog pups

Amazing! Dogs can't sweat!
Unlike you, dogs don't have
sweat glands, so they can't
lose heat
through
their skin.
They pant
when they
get hot, to
let heat
escape from
their bodies.

Saint
Bernard

What do pups eat?

Newborn wild pups live
off mother's milk. Soon, their
mum brings them meat. She
chews it for them, until they're
a bit bigger. Finally at four
months old, the pups are old
enough to join in the hunt.

Which is the biggest dog?

The grey wolf is biggest wild dog and the most powerful. Males can be as long as six feet and weigh up to 175 pounds, as much as four six-year-old children! Some grey wolves have brown, red or black coats.

Grey wolf

Amazing!
Except for the African wild dog, all pet dogs are descended from a wolf-like ancestor, which appeared about one million years ago.

Do wolves howl at the Moon?

Wolves howl whether the Moon's out or not. They use their powerful voices to tell other packs of wolves to stay away, and to talk to members of their own pack, especially when they have spread out to hunt.

 Is it true?
You should never try to out-stare a wolf.

No. You should if you're a musk ox. Wolves usually hunt by picking off young or sick members of a group of grazing animals. Musk oxen try to stop this happening by huddling in a tight circle. Faced with a wall of horns, the Arctic wolves can't pick off any individual oxen.

 ## Which wolf walks on stilts?

The maned wolf is the tallest wild dog. Its legs are longer than the length of its body! The maned wolf lives in the grasslands of South America. Its stilts give it a good view over the tall Pampas grasses.

Maned wolf

Which is the biggest bear?

The powerful polar bear weighs in at 1,320 pounds, which makes it about ten times heavier than a grown-up person, and the biggest of all meat-eating land mammals. Adult bears snack on fish and seals, but they have even been spotted guzzling down fat beluga whales that weigh as much as themselves!

 Amazing! Polar bears cover their nose with their paw when they hunt. Although their fur is white, their noses are black and easy to spot in the snow. By covering its nose, the polar bear makes sure that its whole body is camouflaged against the snowy Arctic landscape.

Polar bear

Which cubs drink the creamiest milk?

Newborn polar bear cubs are tiny. They need to fatten up quickly to survive the cold. Luckily, their mother's milk is thick and creamy and about half of it is pure fat.

Polar bear cubs

Can bears walk on water?

They can when it's frozen! Polar bears roam across northern Europe, northern Asia and North America. If the Arctic Ocean isn't frozen they swim, protected by thick fur and fat!

Is it true?
Polar bears poisoned Arctic explorers.

Yes. Polar bears' livers contain a lot of Vitamin A. In small doses, this is fine for humans, but when hungry explorers ate the livers, they were poisoned.

Which bear fishes for its supper?

The brown bear is a top angler. It knows just the time of year that delicious salmon head upriver to lay their eggs. The bear catches the fish with a quick swipe of the paw, or it waits until the salmon leap up mini waterfalls, and become tired.

Brown bear

Brown bear cub

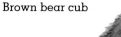

 When do bears climb trees?

When they want to escape danger. Black bears are expert climbers even as grown-ups. Brown bears only climb trees when they are cubs, usually to escape from adult brown bears, who are trying to eat them!

Amazing! The American black bear is one of the world's champion snoozers. Its winter sleep, or hibernation, lasts for seven months – over half of the year!

 Is it true?
Koalas are bears.

No. Although we call them koala bears, koalas are really marsupials, which means they have pouches like kangaroos. Pandas aren't bears either. They're more closely related to raccoons.

 Do all bears eat meat?
Even meat-eating bears sometimes like a change of diet. Polar bears snack on seaweed and berries when seals are scarce. Brown and black bears love honey, but collecting it is a very risky business. They often come away from the hive with a stung nose!

Giant panda

CHAPTER FIFTEEN
WHALES
AND OTHER SEA MAMMALS

Dugong

What are sea mammals?

Sea mammals spend most of their lives in or near the sea. There are three groups of sea mammals. Whales and dolphins are called cetaceans. Seals and walruses are called pinnipeds. Manatees and dugongs are called sirenians.

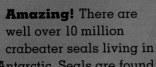

Amazing! There are well over 10 million crabeater seals living in the icy Antarctic. Seals are found in many parts of the world, but the southern crabeaters are the most common type of seal on Earth.

Blue whale

Whale's blowholes

Which special features help whales live in the sea?
A whale's body is designed for swimming. It has a smooth, streamlined shape for pushing through the water, and blowholes for breathing on top of its head.

Which is the biggest sea mammal?
The huge blue whale is the biggest mammal in the sea. In fact, it's the biggest animal that has ever lived. It can grow more than 100 feet long and weigh as much as 130 tons.

Is it true?
Whales once lived on land.

Yes. The ancestors of today's whales once lived on land. About 50 million years ago, they went into the sea to look for food and their bodies adapted to life in the water.

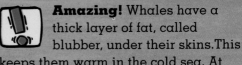 **Amazing!** Whales have a thick layer of fat, called blubber, under their skins. This keeps them warm in the cold sea. At about 20 inches, the bowhead whale has the thickest blubber.

 Do all whales have teeth?

Some whales have long, tough bristles, called baleen, hanging down inside their mouths, instead of teeth. They don't chew their food, but sieve it from the water through the baleen.

Baleen whale

 Is it true?
A whale uses its blowhole as a nose.

Yes. Like all mammals, whales must breathe air to stay alive. Instead of nostrils, they have a blowhole on top of the head.

Close up of barnacles

Barnacles

What has tiny shellfish on its back?

Some whales have tonnes of tiny shellfish growing on their backs. The shellfish are called barnacles. They need to have a solid surface to glue their shells on to. Any rock, ship or passing whale will do.

Dolphin

What's the difference between whales and dolphins?

Strictly speaking, dolphins are small whales with sharp, pointed teeth for catching food. Dolphins live in seas all over the world. The biggest dolphin is the killer whale.

What do walruses use their tusks for?

A walrus uses its long tusks to chip shellfish from rocks and break breathing holes in the ice. The males also use their tusks to fight off rivals and attract a mate.

Walruses

Hooded seal

Which seal blows up balloons?

To attract a mate or scare off a rival, a male hooded seal blows air into its nose! It can inflate the lining of one of its nostrils so that it looks like a big, red balloon.

Is it true?

Seals cry when they are sad.

No. Seals sometimes look as if they're crying, but it's not because they're sad. The tears keep their eyes moist and clean. In the sea, they get washed away. On land, they trickle down their cheeks.

Weddell seal

Which seals live at the ends of the Earth?

Weddell seals live in the far south, on ice-covered islands off the coast of freezing Antarctica. Ringed seals live in the Arctic, at the other end of the world. They've been found as far north as the North Pole.

Amazing! In hot weather, some seals and sealions flip tiny pebbles and sand on to their backs with their flippers. This helps to keep them cool, and it also scratches them if their skin is feeling itchy.

Which sea mammal can swim the fastest?

The fastest sea mammal in the world is the killer whale. With its streamlined body and powerful tail, it can speed through the water at up to 35 mph. That's more than six times faster than the quickest human swimmers.

Sperm whale

Is it true?
Spinner dolphins spin like tops in the air.

Yes. Spinner dolphins are easy to recognize. They can leap out of the water, high into the air, then spin around quickly like tops. These amazing acrobats live near the coast in warm seas.

Sea lion

Which is the speediest seal?

The fastest seal in the sea is the California sea lion, with a top speed of 25 mph. The fastest on land is the crabeater seal, reaching 12 mph over snow and ice.

 Amazing! Some sea mammals can hold their breath for almost two hours before they have to come to the surface for air. Most humans can only hold their breath for a minute or so.

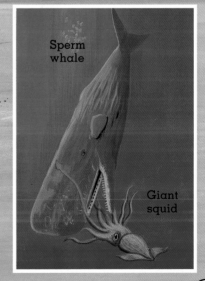
Sperm whale

Giant squid

 ## What is one of the deepest divers?

Sperm whales dive over a mile after their food. One sperm whale was even found with two deep-sea sharks in its stomach. It must have dived to nearly two miles to catch them.

Which whales turn somersaults in the air?

Humpback whales are very athletic. Even though the whales may weigh 65 tons, they can leap high into the air and come crashing down into the water on their backs. They can even turn somersaults in the air.

Humpback whale

Amazing! In the Arctic and Antarctic, seals dive under the ice to search for food. They can hold their breath for up to 30 minutes before they need to come up for air, so they chew breathing holes in the ice with their strong front teeth.

 Which sea mammals walk with their teeth?

A walrus's tusks are actually its two upper teeth. They grow up to three feet long. The walrus uses its tusks to pull itself out of the sea and drag itself across the land.

Walrus

Gray whale

 Which sea mammals make the longest journey?

Gray whales spend the summers feeding in the Arctic. In winter, they swim to the coast of Mexico to breed. They swim back north again in the spring, a round trip of about 12,500 miles.

Is it true?
Whales slap their tails against the sea surface because they're angry.

No. Some whales slap their huge tails down on the water but it's not because they're angry. This is called 'lobtailing' and it's probably a signal to other whales.

Which are the most intelligent sea mammals?

Dolphins are quick to learn tricks and remember instructions. This makes them very popular with people. They are also friendly and sociable. Many dolphins live in large groups. They play and hunt for food together.

Which seal has a huge nose?

The male northern elephant seal gets its name from its very long nose, which normally hangs down over its mouth. It can inflate its nose, like a balloon, to attract a mate.

Northern elephant seal

Dolphin

Is it true?
Beluga whales are called 'sea canaries' because of their yellow skin.

No. Beluga whales whistle and chirp just like singing birds, such as canaries. In fact, they make so much noise, they're nicknamed 'sea canaries'. Adult belugas have pure white skin.

Humpback whales

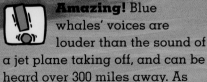

Amazing! Blue whales' voices are louder than the sound of a jet plane taking off, and can be heard over 300 miles away. As well as being the biggest animals, blue whales are the noisiest creatures in the world!

Why do whales sing to each other?

Whales build sounds into 'songs' which can last for ten minutes or more. The whales sing to keep in touch with each other, to find a mate and to frighten off rivals.

Baleen

Which whale has the longest 'teeth'?

All of the great whales, such as the blue whale have hundreds of bony baleen, which they use to sieve food from the water. The Bowhead whale's baleen are up to 13 feet long.

Is it true?
Leopard seals are fussy eaters.

No. Leopard seals eat almost anything, including penguins, sea birds, fish, squid, seal pups, and even duck-billed platypuses!

Leopard seal

How do leopard seals catch their prey?

Leopard seals mainly eat penguins. To catch them, the seals build up speed in the water, then launch themselves on to the ice. They have even been known to snap at human divers, probably because they mistake them for penguins.

Blue whale

 Which sea mammal has the biggest appetite?

Blue whales have massive appetites. In spring and summer, they eat up to four tons of krill (tiny, shrimp-like creatures) each day. That's about five times as much food as you eat each year!

Amazing! Whales and dolphins can shut off their windpipes when they're underwater. They do this when they're feeding. It stops water from passing into their lungs and making them choke.

Which are the biggest sea mammal babies?

When a baby blue whale is born, it weighs between two and three tons. It drinks about 105 pints of its mother's milk a day, and by seven months old, it weighs 20 tons!

Amazing! Every year, a herd of about 1.5 million fur seals gather on the Pribilof Islands in Alaska to breed. What a squash!

Blue whale and calf

Which sea mammals live in a pod?

Some dolphins live in family groups called pods. A pod may be hundreds of dolphins strong. The dolphins help each other out. If one of them is ill, for example, the others look after it, by pushing it to the surface so that it can breathe.

Pod of dolphins

Which sea mammals live the longest?

Whales and dolphins have long lives. Fin whales probably live the longest, between 90 and 100 years. The Baird's beaked whale is close behind. It can live for up to 80 years.

Fin whale

 Is it true?

Baby whales and dolphins are born head first.

No. A baby whale or dolphin is born tail first. Otherwise it might drown. Its mother pushes it to the surface so that it can take its first breath.

Which seal pups were hunted for their coats?

Harp seal pups are born with soft, white fur coats. They lose these after a month and grow dark coats like adult seals. In the past, thousands of pups were killed for their fur.

Harp seal pup

Amazing! Steller's sea cows were huge dugongs that once lived in the Bering Sea. They were discovered in 1741. Just 30 years later, they were extinct because so many had been eaten by sailors.

Why are sea mammals in danger?

People are very dangerous for sea mammals. They hunt seals and whales for their meat, fur and blubber, and they trap sea mammals, such as dolphins, in fishing nets. Many more mammals are poisoned by pollution, such as oil from tankers, which is dumped into the sea.

 Is it true?
Right whales are easy to hunt.

Yes. Right whales were once the right whales to hunt. They swam slowly and floated on the surface when they were killed.

Whale hunt

Gulf porpoises

 ## Which are the rarest sea mammals?

There are fewer than 600 Mediterranean monk seals left, but the rarest sea mammal is probably the Gulf porpoise. There may be only 50 left off the Californian coast.

Elephant seal

 Amazing! Most whales and dolphins are able to snooze for a few minutes while they're swimming or resting on the sea floor. But it's thought that the Dall's porpoise never goes to sleep at all.

 ## Which is the biggest seal?

Antarctic southern elephant seals are the biggest seals. Male seals grow up to 20 feet long, measure almost 13 feet around the middle and weigh in at about three tons.

 Is it true? Sperm whales have the heaviest mammal brains.

Yes. A sperm whale's brain weighs up to 20 pounds. That's about six times heavier than a human brain! Luckily, the whale has a very large head to fit it in, which takes up about a third of its body.

Which whale is the tiniest?

The smallest whale is probably the Commerson's dolphin. This miniature mammal grows about three feet long. It would take about 3,000 dolphins to make up the weight of one blue whale.

Commerson's dolphin

Which whale has the tallest 'blow'?

The 'blow' is the spout of water you see when a whale breathes out. The gigantic blue whale has the tallest blow. It can reach a height of 40 feet, as high as six tall people. Each whale makes a different pattern as it blows.

Blue whale

CHAPTER SIXTEEN
GORILLAS
AND OTHER PRIMATES

Spider
monkey

How do you tell a monkey from an ape?

By looking at its bottom! If it has no tail, it's probably either a 'great ape' – a gorilla, chimp, orang-utan, or bonobo – or it might be a type of gibbon or 'lesser ape', such as the siamang. Except for a few out of over 100 types, monkeys do have tails. Monkeys and apes belong to a group of intelligent animals called primates.

Gorilla

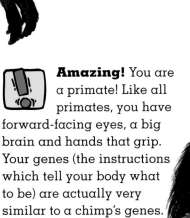

 Amazing! You are a primate! Like all primates, you have forward-facing eyes, a big brain and hands that grip. Your genes (the instructions which tell your body what to be) are actually very similar to a chimp's genes.

Hedgehog

 ## Who's stopped being a primate?

Experts used to say that the tree shrew was a primate, but really they're more similar to insect-eating creatures such as moles, shrews and hedgehogs.

 ## Are monkeys and apes the only primates?

Lemurs, bushbabies, lorises and tarsiers are all primitive primates. They have smaller brains than monkeys or apes and rely more on their sense of smell than sight.

Slender loris

Tarsier

Crowned lemur

 ### Is it true?

Primates were around in dinosaur days.

Yes. People have found fossils of early, squirrel-sized primates that lived about 70 million years ago – about the same time that terrifying Tyrannosaurus rex roamed the land.

Which ape has the longest arms?

In relation to its overall size, the orang-utan has the biggest armspan. Its arms are three times as long as its body, which is just right for an animal that spends its life swinging from tree to tree! The name orang-utan is the Malay for 'man of the woods'.

Orang-utan

Is it true?
Gorillas in the wild are bigger than gorillas in zoos.

No. Life in a zoo can make gorillas rather lazy and, sometimes, rather fat! The record-breaker was a male called N'gagi, who weighed in at a whopping 682 pounds. That's about the same as five adult humans!

Which is the most colorful monkey?

Male mandrills, which belong to the baboon family, have very brightly colored faces. Mandrills are also among the biggest monkeys, at just under three feet tall, with a weight of about 44 pounds.

Mandrill

Amazing! The gorilla is the world's biggest ape. It is a tiny bit taller than a man, but usually about three times as heavy.

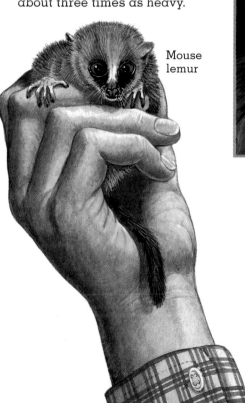

Mouse lemur

Which is the world's smallest primate?

The eastern brown mouse lemur of Madagascar is truly tiny. From the top of its head to its bottom, it measures just over two inches. It could easily sit on your palm, if it wasn't so shy!

Gorilla

Is it true?
Gorillas are monster meat-eaters.

No.
Despite their enormous size, these gentle giants are vegetarians. They feed on fruits, roots and vegetables, especially delicious wild celery.

Where do gorillas sleep?

It's not just birds that sleep in nests – huge gorillas do too! They bend branches in bushes and trees and make a cozy bed just above the ground. Sometimes they make a mini day nest, where they snatch a midday snooze.

324

Which gorillas go gray?

Adult male gorillas are called silverbacks, because of the silvery gray fur on their back and face. The silverback is the leader, who defends the troop.

Silverback gorilla

Amazing! Gorillas use sign language! Wild gorillas communicate with grunts and body language. But a gorilla called Koko learned proper sign language, as used by people who can't speak or hear.

When is it rude to stare?

It's always rude to look straight at a gorilla. In gorilla language, staring means you're angry and looking for a fight. Sometimes, gorillas beat their chests when they're cross.

What ate 500 figs in a single week?

All lemurs love to come across a tree of juicy figs, but one ruffed lemur once ate about 500 figs in a week. The greedy lemur defended the crop of fruit against any would-be raiders!

Ruffed lemur

 **Is it true?**
Tarsiers have a swivelling head.

Yes. Tarsiers can turn their head half a full circle, like an owl. This is a perfect way to catch an unsuspecting katydid or other flying insect.

 ## Do monkeys and apes eat bananas?

Primates do eat bananas and even peel them first. Fruit, seeds, flowers, shoots, leaves and fungi (types of mushroom) are all perfect primate meals. The orang-utan's favorite snack is the stinky durian fruit, which smells like cheese.

Baby orang-utan

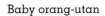

Amazing! Primates chew gum. Many primates, especially marmosets and bushbabies, scrape away the bark of a gum tree to get at the sap. But when it's fresh the gum is liquid, so the animals drink rather than chew.

Which primates eat poison?
Lorises eat insects that are so toxic (poisonous) that they would give other animals a heart attack! They sneak up on their prey and grab it with their hands. The golden bamboo lemur even eats young bamboo shoots that contain cyanide, which is a very dangerous poison.

Slow loris

Ring-tailed lemur

How do lemur babies get around?

Like all primates, newborn lemur babies cling to their mum's tum as she moves about the forest. As they get bigger and more curious, they have a piggyback, to get a better view.

Is it true?
Only mums look after primate babies.

No. Baby titis are looked after by dad, and young male baboons often borrow a baby. No older male will attack, in case they harm the baby!

Do primate babies drink milk?

Primates are mammals – they give birth to live young and feed them milk. Most primates, including humans, usually have one baby at a time, but marmosets usually have twins.

Baby orang-utan

 Amazing! Baby gibbons wear bonnets. When it's born, a baby gibbon has a cap of fur on the top of its head. Just like human babies, the rest of the baby gibbon's body is completely bare!

Baby orang-utans

 ## Why are monkeys so cheeky?

All young monkeys love to play and it's as important as school is for you! This is how they learn the skills they will need when they grow up.

Which is the noisiest primate?

The howler monkey is well-named, because it makes a terrific noise that can be heard up to three miles away through the trees. They hold howling competitions with neighboring groups, to remind each other to keep to their own part of the forest.

Amazing! Monkeys do sentry duty. When a troop is enjoying a feast, one or two animals keep a lookout for predators. They have many different warning calls. For example, they make a certain noise only if a leopard is nearby.

Howler monkeys

Who grins with fright?
Chimpanzees have a special fear grin. They use it to warn others of danger without making a giveaway noise. Sometimes, when chimps come face to face with a predator, they use the horrible grin to try to frighten it away.

Bushbaby

Is it true?
Bushbabies rub wee on their feet!

Yes. And they also rub wee on their hands! It's their way of leaving lots of smelly graffiti on the trees. Every place they've gripped has a scent which says 'we were here'.

Mandrill

Whose bottom has something to say?
Many primates have brightly-colored bottoms which are easy to see in the dim forest light. These bottoms tell other members of their own kind where they are. The mandrill's bottom is the most colorful – it's bright blue and red!

Who's the king of the swingers?

Gibbons are the champion swingers. They have special bones in their wrists and shoulders to give them plenty of swing as they move from tree to tree. These long-armed apes live in the tropical forests of Malaysia and Indonesia.

Amazing! Primates have their own cushions. Many primates, including baboons which spend a lot of time sitting around, have built-in padding on their backsides.

Spider monkey

What hangs by the tail?

Woolly monkeys, spider monkeys and howler monkeys all have a bare patch of tail for extra grip. They are the only primates that can support all their weight with the tail and hang upside-down.

Silvery
gibbons

 Is it true?
Slow lorises really
do move slowly.

Yes. Lorises are the most
relaxed primates. Unlike
their busy monkey cousins,
lorises stroll very slowly
through the forest in
search of food.

 **When are two legs
better than four?**
Crossing open ground can be a
dangerous business with
predators about. Lemurs can
travel much more quickly on
two legs than four. Standing
upright also gives them a
better view, and frees up their
front legs, to pick up food.

Lemur

Amazing! Chimps take medicine. Chimpanzees sometimes eat plants that don't taste very nice at all, as cures for illness. One herbal remedy is aspilia, which gets rid of tummy upsets and worms.

Gorilla painting

Which ape uses tools?

Chimps are very clever, and even make simple tools. They sometimes strip a stick of its bark to make a kind of fishing rod that they use to fish for termites. They also use sticks to gather honey so they needn't get too close to the nest and risk a nasty bee sting!

Termite mound

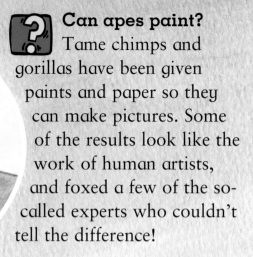

Can apes paint?

Tame chimps and gorillas have been given paints and paper so they can make pictures. Some of the results look like the work of human artists, and foxed a few of the so-called experts who couldn't tell the difference!

Is it true?

Chimps can talk.

No. People have taught chimps to point at symbols and to use sign language, so we know that they are clever enough to understand language. But chimps' vocal cords are unable to produce spoken words like ours.

Who carries a pet stone?

Chimpanzees who live on Mount Tai, in West Africa, use a stone as a nutcracker to smash open the hard shells of the coula nut. There aren't many rocks on the mountain, so each chimp carries around its own favorite stone.

Chimpanzee

 Amazing! Some people think that there are primates yet to be discovered – abominable snowmen! There are many tales of monstrous primates in remote parts of the world, including the yeti from central Asia.

Emperor tamarin

 Should people keep primates in zoos?
Primates are happiest in the wild, but zoos do important work. They breed animals that are becoming endangered, such as the golden lion tamarin or the silvery marmoset. Zoos also help people to learn about their ape and monkey cousins. This helps people to understand better why primates should be protected in the wild.

Golden lion tamarin

Why are primates in danger?

Not all primates are threatened, but some are. Some, such as the emperor tamarin with its beautiful whiskery moustache, are caught to be sold as pets. Gorillas and orang-utans are in danger because people are destroying their habitat and are also hunting them. There are only about 650 gorillas left in the wild.

Bamboo lemur

Is it true?
People eat chimp and chips.

No. A few apes and monkeys are caught for food, but the biggest threats are the pet trade and the destruction of the places where they live.

Which primate came back from the dead?

Sometimes primates are thought to be extinct, only to re-appear. This happened with the greater bamboo lemur. Most primates are shy and good at hiding. Also, they often live in remote places which are difficult to explore.

CHAPTER SEVENTEEN
OUR SOLAR SYSTEM

What is the Solar System?

Solar means 'of the Sun'. The Solar System is centered around the Sun, the shining ball in the sky. It includes the family of nine planets orbiting (traveling around) the Sun, as well as the moons of these planets, and smaller objects, such as comets, asteroids, and bits of space rock. The powerful pull of an invisible force called gravity from the Sun stops these bodies from flying off into deepest space.

Saturn
Distance from Sun
885 million miles
Diameter 80,389 miles

Mars
Distance from Sun
141 million miles
Diameter 4,214 miles

Earth
Distance from Sun
93 million miles
Diameter 7,909 miles

Mercury
Distance from Sun
36 million miles
Diameter 3.024 miles

Venus
Distance from Sun
67 million miles
Diameter 7,504 miles

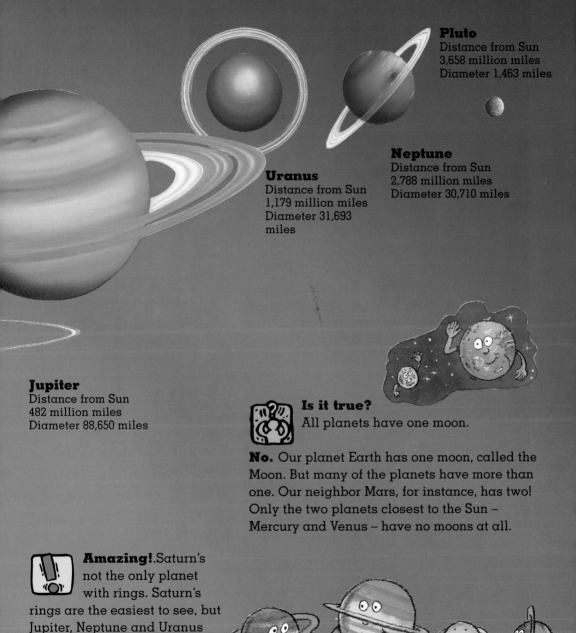

Pluto
Distance from Sun
3,658 million miles
Diameter 1,463 miles

Neptune
Distance from Sun
2,788 million miles
Diameter 30,710 miles

Uranus
Distance from Sun
1,179 million miles
Diameter 31,693
miles

Jupiter
Distance from Sun
482 million miles
Diameter 88,650 miles

Is it true?
All planets have one moon.

No. Our planet Earth has one moon, called the
Moon. But many of the planets have more than
one. Our neighbor Mars, for instance, has two!
Only the two planets closest to the Sun –
Mercury and Venus – have no moons at all.

Amazing!.Saturn's
not the only planet
with rings. Saturn's
rings are the easiest to see, but
Jupiter, Neptune and Uranus
have them, too. Saturn has
seven main rings, and then
hundreds of thinner rings,
called ringlets.

How hot is the Sun?

In deserts here on Earth, heat that has traveled 93 million miles from the Sun can be hot enough to fry an egg. The Sun's surface is a super-hot 10,832°F, and its centre or core is even hotter.

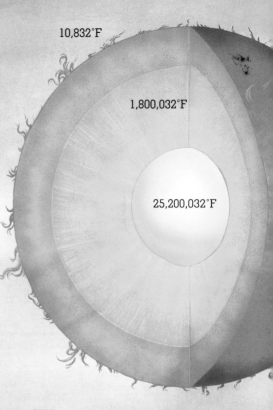

10,832°F

1,800,032°F

25,200,032°F

 Amazing!
The Sun is a star – a gigantic ball of burning gas. It has been shining for about five billion years.

Why must you never look at the Sun?

Not even sunglasses fully protect your eyes from the Sun's dangerous ultraviolet (UV) rays. UV can burn your eyes and make you blind. If you want to see the Sun safely, ask an adult to show you how to project its image on to a sheet of paper.

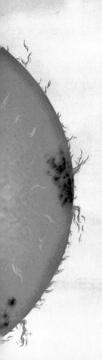

Is it true?
The Sun has spots.

Yes. The Sun is not the same color all over. Some areas of its surface are darker. These spots are little pockets that are slightly cooler. Of course, sunspots are only 'little' compared to the Sun – some grow to be as large as Jupiter, the biggest planet in the Solar System!

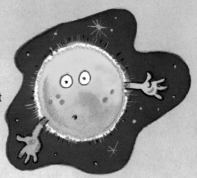

WARNING!
Never look at the Sun, even if you're wearing sunglasses.

When does the Sun go out?
When there's a total eclipse. This happens when the Moon's path takes it between the Earth and the Sun, and the Moon casts a shadow across the surface of the Earth.

Total eclipse of the Sun

What does Mercury look like?

Planet Mercury looks very like our Moon. It's about the same size and it's covered in craters, where bits of space rock have crash-landed on its surface. The biggest crater is the Caloris Basin, which is about 800 miles across. Mercury also has huge plains, rolling hills, deep gorges, chasms, and cliffs.

Earth

Mercury

Is it true?
Mercury is the smallest planet.

No. Mercury is only about a third the size of the Earth, but Pluto is even smaller. If you could put them on the scales, it would take 21 Plutos to balance one Mercury.

The surface of Mercury is covered with craters.

344

 Is Mercury the hottest planet?
Mercury is the planet closest to the Sun, but its neighbor Venus is even hotter, because it has clouds to keep in the heat.

The surface of Mercury is 660°F during the day, and minus 270°F at night.

 What is the weather like on Mercury?

Mercury doesn't have any weather, because it has no air and hardly any atmosphere. That means there are no clouds to shield the surface of the planet from the baking-hot Sun during the day, or to keep in the heat at night. There is no wind or rain on Mercury, either.

Amazing!. Mercury is the fastest planet. Mercury zooms around the Sun in just 88 days, at an incredible 107,000 mph. That makes it faster than any space rocket ever invented.

The planet Venus seen close to the Moon

When is a star not a star?

When it's a planet! Venus is sometimes called the 'evening star' because it's so bright it's one of the first points of light we see shining as it gets dark. Planets don't make their own light – they reflect the Sun's light.

Is it true?
Venus is bigger than the Earth.

No. Venus is a fraction smaller than the Earth, but not by much. Venus is about 7,504 miles across, whereas Earth is about 405 miles wider. Venus's mass is about four-fifths of Earth's.

Earth

Venus

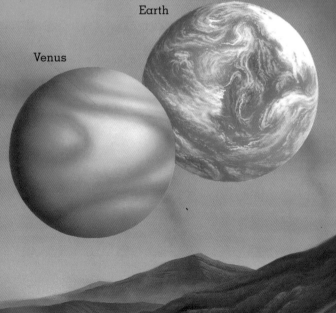

How can a day be longer than a year?

A day is the amount of time a planet takes to spin on its axis, and a year is the time it takes to travel around the Sun. Venus spins on its axis very slowly, but orbits the Sun more quickly than Earth. A day on Venus lasts 243 Earth-days, but a year is only 225 Earth-days.

Volcanic eruption on Venus

What's special about our planet?

As far as we know, Earth is the only planet in the Solar System that has life. As well as warmth from the Sun, the other main ingredient for life is liquid water. Earth has plenty of water – in total, it covers about three-quarters of the planet's surface!

Earth seen from space

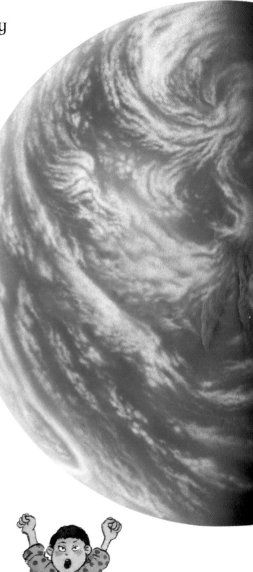

Is it true?
There was life on Earth from the start.

No. When Earth first formed it was extremely hot and there was no oxygen. Over millions of years, the planet cooled, oceans formed and oxygen was made. The first life on Earth appeared about 3 billion years ago.

What does Earth look like from space?

It looks beautiful – blue with swirling white clouds. Astronauts in space spend most of their free time gazing at it. They can even make out cities, when they are lit up at night with twinkling lights.

Amazing! The Earth is magnetic. At the center of the Earth is a core of a molten metal called iron, which makes our planet like a giant magnet. This is what pulls the needle on a compass towards the magnetic North Pole.

Why does our sky go dark at night?

Like all planets, the Earth is spinning as it orbits the Sun. When your part of the planet is facing away from the Sun, its light is blocked out. At the same time, it is daytime for people on the opposite side of the Earth.

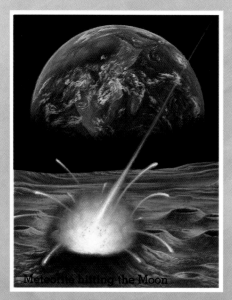
Meteorite hitting the Moon

 Why does the Moon have so many craters?
Because it has been pelted by so many space rocks and has no atmosphere to protect it. One of the biggest craters, called Bailly, is nearly 190 miles across. You can make out some of the craters using a good pair of binoculars.

New Moon   Crescent Moon   First quarter Moon   Gibbous Moon

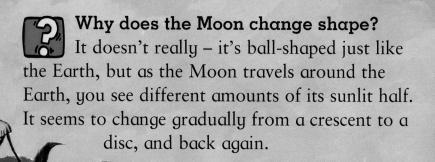 **Why does the Moon change shape?**
It doesn't really – it's ball-shaped just like the Earth, but as the Moon travels around the Earth, you see different amounts of its sunlit half. It seems to change gradually from a crescent to a disc, and back again.

Amazing! You can jump higher on the Moon. The Moon's gravity is much weaker than Earth's. This means you would only weigh about a sixth of your Earth-weight there – and you'd be able to jump six times higher!

 ## What is the dark side of the Moon?

It's the part of the Moon that we can never see from Earth. The Moon takes the same time to orbit the Earth as it does to spin once. This means the same side of the Moon always faces away from the Earth.

Full Moon

 ### Is it true?
There are seas on the Moon.

Yes and no. There are dark, rocky plains and craters called maria (Latin for 'seas'), but they don't contain water. The first astronauts to visit the Moon landed on the Sea of Tranquility.

Earth

Mars

Which is the red planet?

Mars was named after the Roman god of war, because of its blood-red color. The planet looks rusty red because its surface is covered with iron-rich soil and rock. There are no seas on Mars, and it is very cold.

Does Mars have ice at its poles?

Yes. Its south pole is mostly 'dry ice', which is frozen carbon dioxide gas. At the north pole there may be frozen water, mixed with the frozen carbon dioxide. There may be frozen water underground on Mars, too.

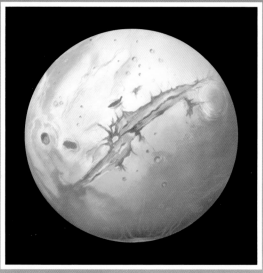

One of Mars's polar caps, at the bottom of the planet

The Martian surface, showing Olympus Mons

Is it true?
There is life on Mars.

No. Or at least, there's no sure sign of any. But long ago, Mars had flowing rivers of water, so there could have been life once, and there may be fossils buried underground.

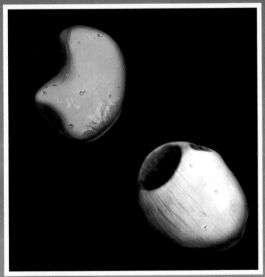

Phobos
(about 9 miles long)

Deimos
(about 17 miles long)

What are Mars's moons like?

Mars's two tiny moons, Deimos and Phobos, are not round like our Moon. They look more like baked potatoes! They might have been asteroids (space rocks) that Mars captured with its gravity.

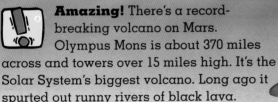
Amazing! There's a record-breaking volcano on Mars. Olympus Mons is about 370 miles across and towers over 15 miles high. It's the Solar System's biggest volcano. Long ago it spurted out runny rivers of black lava.

William Herschel

Which planet was found by accident?

Uranus was discovered in 1781. The man who found it, William Herschel, was not expecting to find a planet at all. He thought he was pointing his homemade telescope at a distant star.

How many moons does Uranus have?

Uranus has at least 17 moons – but there could be more to discover. They are all named after characters from English literature. The main ones are Oberon, Titania, Umbriel, Ariel and Miranda. Ophelia and Cordelia are the closest.

Miranda

Amazing! The poles on Uranus are warmer than the equator. Because Uranus is tilted on its side, the poles are the warmest places on the planet. Summer at the south pole lasts 42 years!

Approaching Uranus through its rings

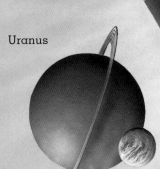

Uranus

Earth

 Why is Uranus blue?
The bluish-green is the color of methane, a stinky gas that makes up part of Uranus's atmosphere. The other gases in the air there are hydrogen and helium – the gas we use to fill party balloons.

Is it true?
Uranus was nearly called George.

Yes. When Herschel discovered the new planet, he wanted to name it after the English king at the time, George III. In the end, it was called Uranus, after the Greek god of the sky.

George

Which planet has pulling power?

Astronomers knew Neptune must be there before they saw it! They could tell something big was pulling Uranus and they were able to predict exactly where Neptune was – almost 2.8 billion miles away from the Sun.

Storm on Neptune

What's the weather like on Neptune?

Very, very windy! Winds rip across the planet all the time, much faster than any winds on Earth. There are also lots of storms on Neptune, which show up as dark spots. This means Neptune's appearance is constantly changing.

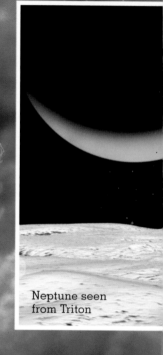

Neptune seen from Triton

Neptune's windy surface

Is it true?
Triton is Neptune's only moon.

No. Neptune has seven other moons, but Triton and Nereid are the main ones. Triton is the biggest. It is 1,678 miles across – about four-fifths the size of our Moon.

Where would you find pink snow?
When the gas nitrogen freezes, it looks like pink snow! There is frozen nitrogen at Neptune's north and south poles, and at the poles of its largest moon, Triton. So far from the Sun, Neptune and its moons are bitterly cold places.

Amazing! Triton is one of the coldest places ever recorded! The temperature on the ice-covered moon is minus 392° F. That's just 98°F away from being the lowest possible temperature in the entire Universe!

357

Pluto's icy surface is minus 220°C

 Which is the coldest planet?
Pluto is the coldest planet of all, which is not surprising, because it is usually the farthest from the Sun. Inside, it is made up of ice and rock, and the planet has a thick layer of ice over the top.

 Is it true?
Pluto was named after a cartoon dog.

No. Pluto was the name of the Greek god of the underworld. Also, the first two letters of Pluto, 'P' and 'L' are the initials of Percival Lowell, who first predicted a planet beyond Neptune.

Who found Pluto's moon?
An American called Jim Christy discovered Pluto's moon in 1978. He called it Charon, which was his wife's name, and also the name of the man who ferried people to the underworld in Ancient Greek mythology.

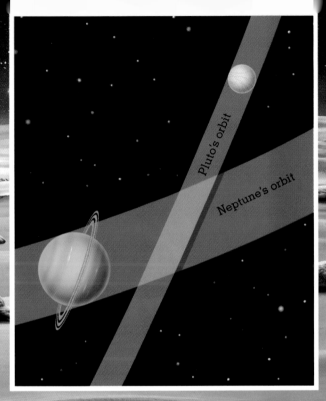

Pluto's orbit

Neptune's orbit

 Amazing! Pluto is smaller than a country. Pluto is a tiny planet – the smallest in the Solar System. At 1,463 miles across, it is smaller than the United States or Russia!

 Is Pluto always farthest from the Sun?

Pluto is so far away from the Sun that it takes 248 years just to orbit it once! But Pluto's orbit is a funny shape. For 20 years of its orbit, Pluto dips in closer to the Sun than Neptune. When this happens, Neptune is the farthest planet in the Solar System.

USA

Pluto

CHAPTER EIGHTEEN
SPACE EXPLORATION

Who made the first rockets?

The Chinese made the first 'rockets' about 1,000 years ago, but they were more like fireworks than today's space rockets. They were flaming arrows that were fired from a basket using gunpowder.

Amazing! You don't need to be a rocket scientist to build rockets. Lots of people make mini rockets as a hobby. There is even a yearly contest, when people show off their latest creations!

Chinese 'rocket'

Is it true?
Thrust SSC is a rocket-powered car.

No. Thrust SSC, the fastest car, has two jet engines. A jet engine could not power a space mission, because it needs air and there's no air in space.

When did the first liquid-fuel rocket fly?

In 1926, American Robert Goddard launched a 11 foot-long rocket. It flew about as high as a two-story house, nowhere near outer space, and landed 184 feet away. The flight lasted just two-and-a-half seconds.

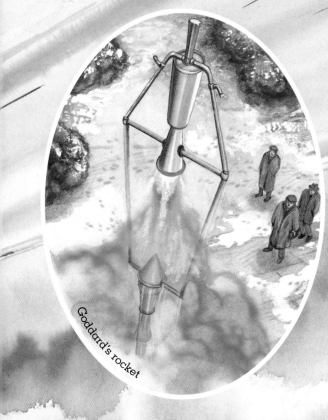

Goddard's rocket

Who built a rocket for war?

Wernher von Braun invented the V2, a rocket missile used by the Germans in World War II. After the war, von Braun moved to the United States, to help with the new American space program.

von Braun and V2 missile

Rockets are important for space travel. They are the only machines powerful enough to launch things into space, such as satellites, probes and people. All the parts needed to build space stations have been carried up by rockets.

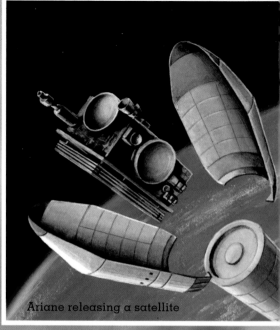
Ariane releasing a satellite

Amazing! The European Ariane rocket could carry a fully-grown elephant. Ariane's biggest payload (cargo) so far was a satellite which weighed 4.6 tons.

How fast can a rocket go?
To escape from Earth's gravity, a rocket has to reach 25,000 mph – almost 20 times faster than supersonic Concorde. Once it is out in space, the rocket drops down to around 18,000 mph to stay in orbit.

Saturn 5 rocket

Is it true?
Saturn 5 rockets were as tall as a 30-story building.

Yes. At 364 feet high, the Saturn 5 was the tallest rocket ever made. Most of the rocket fell away once it had done its job.

 Why do rockets fall to pieces?

Rockets are made in stages, or pieces. Usually, there are three stages, made up of the fuel and rocket engines. Each stage drops off when its job is done. It takes a huge amount of power to push a heavy rocket into space.

Rocket stages falling away

365

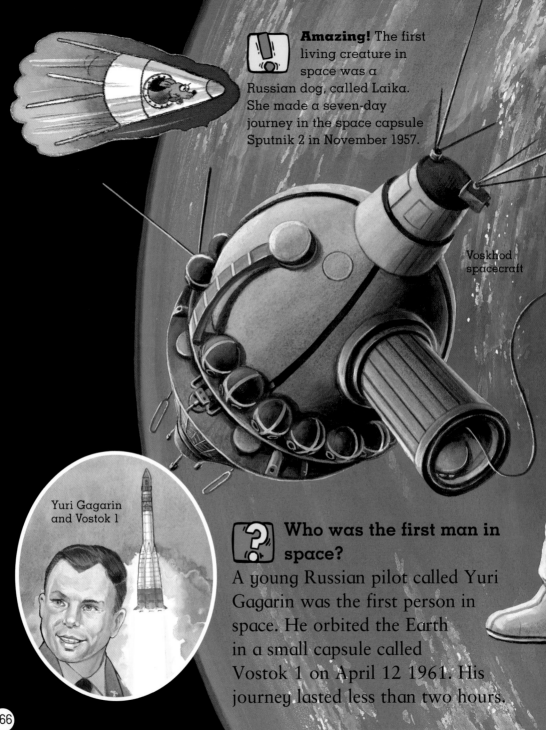

Amazing! The first living creature in space was a Russian dog, called Laika. She made a seven-day journey in the space capsule Sputnik 2 in November 1957.

Voskhod spacecraft

Yuri Gagarin and Vostok 1

Who was the first man in space?

A young Russian pilot called Yuri Gagarin was the first person in space. He orbited the Earth in a small capsule called Vostok 1 on April 12 1961. His journey lasted less than two hours.

Who was the first woman in space?

The first woman in space was Russian, too. Valentina Tereshkova made a three-day space journey in Vostok 6 in 1963. The first American woman in space was Sally Ride, in 1983.

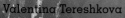
Valentina Tereshkova

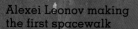
Alexei Leonov making the first spacewalk

Is it true?
A chimp could survive a space flight.

Yes. Ham was the first to try out the Mercury capsule in 1961. Despite traveling at 5,000 mph, the chimpanzee survived the 16-minute flight.

Who took the first spacewalk?

The cosmonaut (Russian astronaut) Alexei Leonov took a ten-minute spacewalk on March 18 1965. To make sure he didn't float off, Leonov tied himself to his capsule.

Neil
Armstrong

 Amazing! There should have been seven manned missions to the Moon. Two days into Apollo 13's journey to the Moon, its oxygen tanks exploded. It took a nail-biting four days to bring its crew safely back to Earth.

 ## Who first set foot on the Moon?

The very first person to step on to the Moon was the American Neil Armstrong, in 1969. He had flown there in Apollo 11 with Buzz Aldrin, who followed him on to the Moon's surface, and Michael Collins.

Apollo 13

 ## How many Moon missions were there?

There were six manned Apollo landings on the Moon, and about 80 unmanned ones too. Apollo 17 landed the last astronauts on the Moon in 1972.

Is it true?
There are footsteps on the Moon.

Yes. There is no atmosphere on the Moon, which means there is no wind either. Tire tracks and footprints in the dusty surface will be there for hundreds of years.

Who first drove on the Moon?
In 1971, Apollo 15 carried a Lunar Rover. David Scott and James Irwin drove the battery-powered buggy over the Moon's cratered surface, collecting samples of Moon rock.

Lunar Rover

？ Why do astronauts wear space suits?

Space suits act like a suit of armor. They stop an astronaut's blood boiling in space, and reflect the Sun's dangerous rays. They have a built-in backpack, containing an oxygen supply, battery and cooling system.

Cutaway of helmet shows communications headset.

Amazing! Astronauts are water-cooled! A system of tubes sewn into the space suit carries cool liquid around to keep the astronaut's temperature normal.

Cutaway of space suit shows water-cooling tubes stitched into undergarment.

Cosmonaut in space capsule

Is it true? Cosmonauts took off in their underwear.

Yes. In the early days of Russian space travel, space suits were worn only for spacewalks. Some cosmonauts just wore their underwear at take-off time!

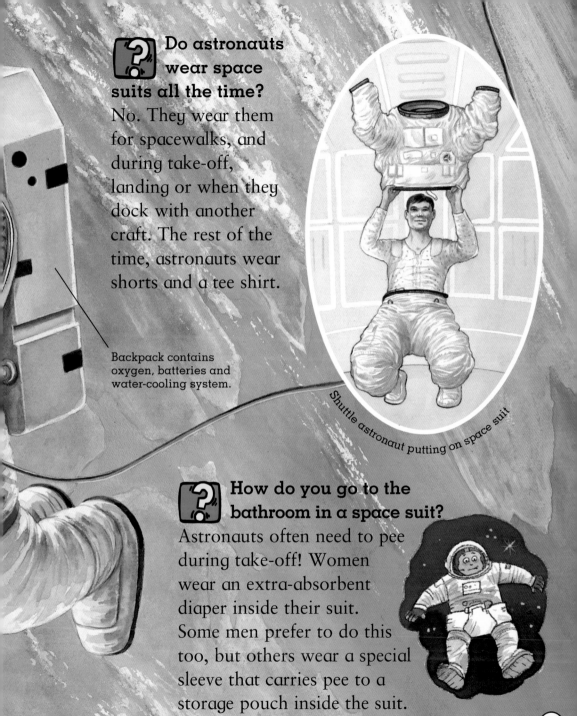

? Do astronauts wear space suits all the time?

No. They wear them for spacewalks, and during take-off, landing or when they dock with another craft. The rest of the time, astronauts wear shorts and a tee shirt.

Backpack contains oxygen, batteries and water-cooling system.

Shuttle astronaut putting on space suit

? How do you go to the bathroom in a space suit?

Astronauts often need to pee during take-off! Women wear an extra-absorbent diaper inside their suit. Some men prefer to do this too, but others wear a special sleeve that carries pee to a storage pouch inside the suit.

What's on the menu in space?

Astronauts either add water to waterless food, or they eat ready meals, such as stew or pasta. Canned fruit, deserts, cookies, candy and gum are all on the menu, too.

Space shuttle galley

Is it true?
Astronauts eat freeze-dried ice cream.

No. The 'astronaut ice cream' sold in the shops isn't really eaten in space. But on the Mir space station, American astronauts took out an ice cream feast to share with the Russian cosmonauts!

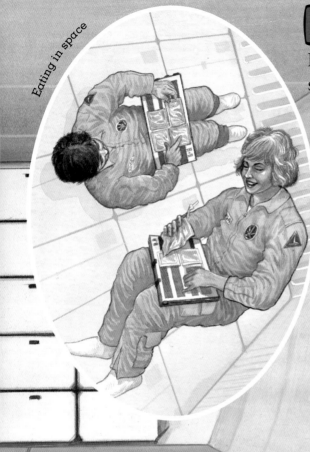
Eating in space

Why doesn't the food float away?
Everything floats about in space, so meals are eaten from trays stuck to astronauts' clothes. Drinks come in a cup with a lid and are sucked up through a straw.

Amazing! Some astronauts get space sickness! Floating makes many astronauts throw up, and if they're not careful the sick flies everywhere! Luckily, the sickness wears off after a day or two.

How do astronauts wash?
The Skylab space station had a shower fitted with a vacuum cleaner to suck off the water, but there's no room for a shower on the shuttle. Astronauts use wet wipes, and clean their hair with rinseless shampoo.

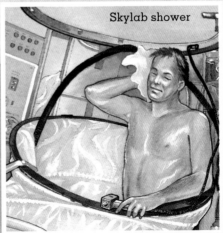
Skylab shower

Has anyone ever been to Mars?

 No, not yet, anyway! The distance from Earth to Mars varies from 35 million miles to 250 million miles. Even at its closest, Mars would be a six-month journey away.

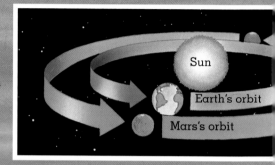

Sun

Earth's orbit

Mars's orbit

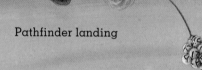

Pathfinder landing

Is it true?
Vikings landed on Mars.

Yes. In 1976, two space probes called Vikings 1 and 2 landed there. During their mission, they collected samples and took over 3,000 photos.

What used balloons to land on Mars?

 The Mars Pathfinder probe entered the Martian atmosphere on July 4 1997. It used a parachute and rockets to slow down and then a bundle of balloons inflated around it so that it could bounce safely down on to the surface.

Amazing! Pathfinder landed in a river! Although there is no liquid water on Mars now, the rocky plain where Pathfinder touched down showed signs that water had flowed there once.

Pathfinder

 Which robot explored Mars?

Pathfinder carried a robot car called Sojourner, which was radio-controlled from Earth. It had a camera and devices for studying the soil and rock.

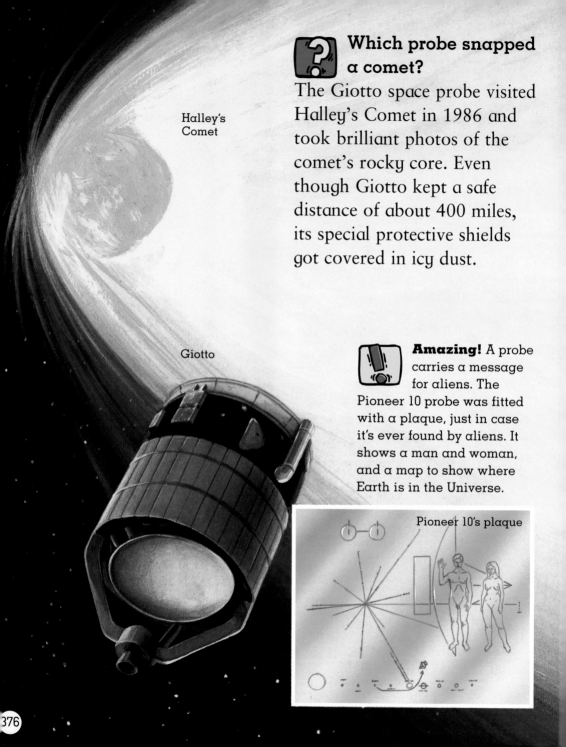

Halley's
Comet

Which probe snapped a comet?

The Giotto space probe visited Halley's Comet in 1986 and took brilliant photos of the comet's rocky core. Even though Giotto kept a safe distance of about 400 miles, its special protective shields got covered in icy dust.

Giotto

Amazing! A probe carries a message for aliens. The Pioneer 10 probe was fitted with a plaque, just in case it's ever found by aliens. It shows a man and woman, and a map to show where Earth is in the Universe.

Pioneer 10's plaque

Is it true?
A probe was made out of junk.

Yes. Magellan, sent to visit Venus in 1989, was made up of spare parts from other missions.

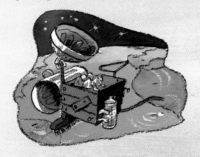

Voyager 2 passing Jupiter

 Which spacecraft flew furthest?

Voyager 2, launched in 1977, has flown past Jupiter, Saturn, Uranus and Neptune. Now it is beyond our Solar System, heading into interstellar space.

Cassini

 Which probe is as big as a bus?

The bus-sized Cassini space probe has another probe, called Huygens, on board. It should reach Saturn in 2004. Cassini will beam data back to Earth about Saturn's rings, moons and the planet itself.

 **Might there be pirates in
space?**
If we ever set up space mining
stations, spacecraft would zoom
about the Solar System with very
valuable cargos. Space pirates
might try to board
cargo-carrying
craft to rob
them!

Moon Base of the future

 ## Will we ever live on the Moon?

There might be a Moon Base, one day. The Moon is only three days away and its low gravity makes it easy to land spacecraft there. It would be a good place for telescopes, because there is no atmosphere to distort the pictures.

 Amazing! People are planning a space hotel. Vacations in space are not far off. There are plans for a doughnut-shaped space hotel, using old shuttle fuel tanks as rooms!

 ## Will we ever live on other planets?

It will take a lot more probe missions before we could consider building bases on other planets. But if travel to other stars ever became possible, the outer planets could act as useful 'gas stations'.

Space tanker near Saturn

CHAPTER NINETEEN
BEYOND OUR SOLAR SYSTEM

What is the Universe?

Every person, planet, star and galaxy is part of the Universe – and even every empty space! The Universe is the biggest thing we have a word for.

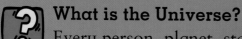

Amazing! The Universe is too big to measure in miles. Even if you could travel at the speed of light, it would take at least 15 billion years to cross it – as far as we know!

 ## What's outside the Universe?

It's impossible to say. Scientists are still trying to guess, by using clues left behind from the birth of our Universe. They are pretty sure there would be no time, distance or things there.

 382

Where are we in the Universe?

People once thought Earth was at the center of the Universe. Now we know Earth is one of many planets moving through space. It's hard to tell where we are because we can't see the Universe's edges.

Our Solar System

Local stars

Our galaxy

Local group of galaxies

Local super group of galaxies

The Universe

Voyager space probe looking at our galaxy in the distant future

Is it true?
There are more stars than people.

Yes. As a rough guess, scientists think that there are about 1.8 million million stars for every human being alive in the world today.

When did the Universe begin?

Scientists have argued about this for centuries. At the moment, most people agree that the Universe began between 12 and 15 billion years ago. It all started with a mind-boggling explosion called the Big Bang.

 Amazing! The Big Bang was super-hot! Scientists don't even bother writing out all the zeros in its temperature. They write $18^{28}°F$, meaning 18 with 28 zeros after it!

 ## What was the Big Bang?

It was a huge explosion, that created all the mass and energy in our Universe in less than a second! The effects of the blast are so strong that the Universe is still expanding.

What if the Big Bang happened again?

It couldn't happen again in our Universe, but some people think it may be happening millions of times, making millions of different universes. Only a few would last as long as ours – most would pop like soap bubbles.

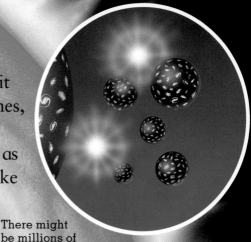

There might be millions of universes.

Is it true?
You could see the Big Bang through a telescope.

Nearly. Our telescopes aren't powerful enough yet – but we can already see light from the other side of the Universe that began its journey just after the Big Bang!

The Universe expands from the Big Bang.

What is the Little Green Man?

LGM stands for 'Little Green Man'. LGM1 is a light deep in space that flashes 30 times a second. It is a pulsar – a tiny, dense neutron star (the remains of a supernova) that flashes out light and radio signals as it spins.

A pulsar flashing out light and radio signals, near a red giant

Is it true?
Scientists thought pulsar signals were messages from aliens.

Yes. The astronomers in Cambridge, England, who discovered LGM1 wondered at first if they'd come across an alien distress beacon or some other kind of coded message!

Amazing!
Neutron stars are super-heavy! They can be just 20 km across, but weigh 50 times more than planet Earth!

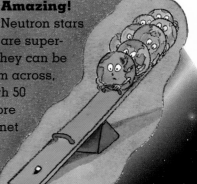

Radio telescopes

How many pulsars are there?

No one is sure, but hundreds have been found since the 1960s, when scientists first spotted the Little Green Man. Special telescopes called radio telescopes are used to 'listen' for more pulsars.

Do all pulsars spin at the same speed?

No – even the slowest spin about once every four seconds, but the fastest whizz round many hundreds of times in a single second! Their incredible speeds are thought to be caused by magnetic forces left by a supernova.

What is a black hole?

A black hole is a place in space that forms when a really huge star collapses. Everything around a black hole is sucked into it, like water down a plug hole. The force of gravity in a black hole is so strong that nothing can escape from it– not even light.

Black hole

Amazing! No one has ever seen a black hole. Because beams of light cannot escape black holes, astronomers cannot see them – even with the most powerful telescopes.

What is dark matter?

Dark matter is what scientists call all the stuff in the Universe that they know is there but can't find! They think it might be made of ghostly little particles called neutrinos.

Neutrinos

 Is it true?
Black holes turn you into spaghetti.

Yes. Scientists think that, in the last moments before you disappeared forever into a black hole, the force of gravity would stretch you until it pulled you apart. They call this being 'spaghettified'!

Dark matter

 ## How do we know that dark matter is there?

Scientists can guess how much matter is in the Universe by measuring how galaxies move. This shows them that stars and planets only make up a small part of the Universe. The rest is invisible!

What is a galaxy?

 A galaxy is a group of stars, dust and gases that are held together by gravity. Our galaxy is the Milky Way and contains about 100 billion stars, one of which is our Sun.

 **Is it true?**
All galaxies have names.

No. Each one that we detect is given numbers and letters, but only some, such as our Milky Way, are given a name as well. 'Galaxy' comes from the Ancient Greek word for 'milk'.

How many galaxies are there?

 No one knows for sure. There might be hundreds of billions of galaxies – and new ones are forming right now at the edges of the Universe.

On a clear night you can see the Milky Way.

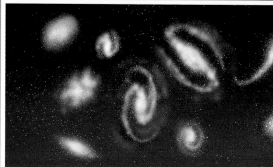

Are there different kinds of galaxies?

Yes – each galaxy is unlike any other. Some are bright and some are dim. There are three basic galaxy shapes, though – spiral, elliptical (oval) and irregular. Of course, irregular just means no particular shape!

Galaxies can form in many weird and wonderful shapes.

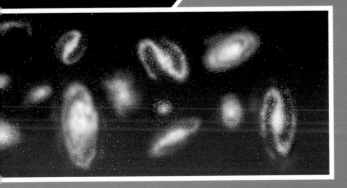

Amazing! There's a galaxy named after a wide-brimmed Mexican hat. 'Sombrero' is the nickname of galaxy M104. Can you guess the galaxy's shape?

391

What shape is our galaxy?

Our galaxy, the Milky Way, is a spiral galaxy. Viewed from above, it looks like a giant Danish pastry with swirls of white icing. From the side, it looks more like two fried eggs stuck back-to-back!

Amazing! Our galaxy has a twin. Andromeda is the biggest galaxy near the Milky Way. It's the same age and a similar shape, but has many more stars.

What's at the middle of the Milky Way?

The center (the two 'egg yolks') is called the nuclear bulge. There's probably a monster black hole there, more than a million times bigger than our Sun. Scientists call the black hole Sagittarius A*.

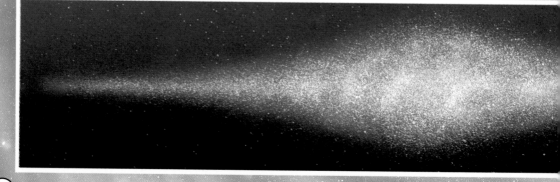

How big is the Milky Way?
The Milky Way is almost too big to imagine. It would take the world's fastest jet, the Blackbird, about 30 billion years to cross the galaxy.

 Is it true?
We're near the center of the Milky Way.

No. Our Solar System is closer to the edge, on one of the spiraling arms. Our Sun takes 225 million years to go around the center once!

Blackbird

A side view of the Milky Way seen from deep space

The Moon's gravity pulls a meteorite crashing into its surface.

Isaac Newton

 What is gravity?
Gravity is one of the basic forces in the Universe, like electromagnetism. It makes things with mass pull towards each other. More massive objects, such as the Earth, pull smaller objects, such as you, towards them until they stick together.

 Is it true?
An apple taught us about gravity.

Maybe. According to legend, super-scientist Isaac Newton first realized how gravity works over 330 years ago, after gravity pulled an apple from a tree he was sitting under, and it landed on his head!

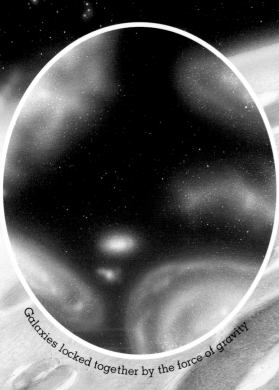

Is the Universe expanding evenly?

No – the force of gravity stops everything from flying outwards. Lumpy bits of space become even lumpier, moving at different speeds. Gravity locks together little pockets of space and matter, such as galaxies.

Galaxies locked together by the force of gravity

Amazing! There are walls in space! Galaxies aren't evenly spaced through the Universe. They are arranged more like walls around emptier regions of space. One wall has already been measured – it's about a billion light years across!

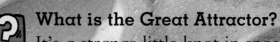

What is the Great Attractor?

It's a strange little knot in space that has the pulling power of 50 million billion Suns, but is not a black hole.

Is time the same everywhere?

No, time slows down when you're traveling very quickly. Brainy boffin Albert Einstein predicted this odd effect in 1905 but we only proved it a few years ago by sending a super-precise atomic clock into orbit around the Earth.

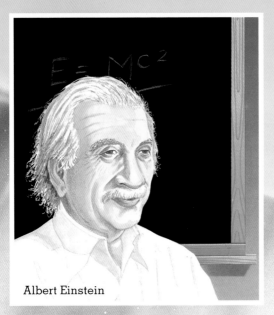

Albert Einstein

 Is it true?
Einstein was the world's best mathematician.

No. Although he was very clever, Albert Einstein often asked his wife to check over the trickier sums for him.

Could time stand still?

Only if you traveled as fast as the speed of light – which most scientists agree is impossible! Some scientists think that time must stand still inside a black hole, but who'd want to find out?

Black hole

Amazing! There might be 'tunnels' through space and time, which connect distant parts of the Universe. Scientists call these shortcuts wormholes. If light or even an object entered a wormhole, perhaps it would pass through incredibly quickly. It would be possible to travel billions of miles in an instant!

Time travel to a different universe

Is time travel possible?

Not as far as we know. If you could invent a machine which seemed to take you back or forwards in time, it would probably be taking you to different universes.

Is there anybody out there?

We don't know. Life might be such a fluke that it only exists on Earth. But if scientists can find just one other place where there is life, we'll know life's no accident – and that there could be millions of aliens!

 How will we find out?

People around the world have joined the Search for Extra-Terrestrial Intelligence (SETI). They spend their spare time on computers, studying waves from space, hoping to find alien messages.

Radio astronomy centre

Do aliens know about us?

It's unlikely. Humans have only been making radio waves for about a century, so aliens would have to live very nearby to tune in.

Amazing! Some people think that the Universe is a living thing – and that the planets, stars and galaxies are just parts of its 'body'!

Aliens with the Pioneer space probe

Is it true?
Aliens have visited the Earth.

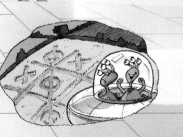

Probably not. There's no proof that aliens have visited us. Even if they could travel at the speed of light, they would take at least four years to reach us from the nearest stars.

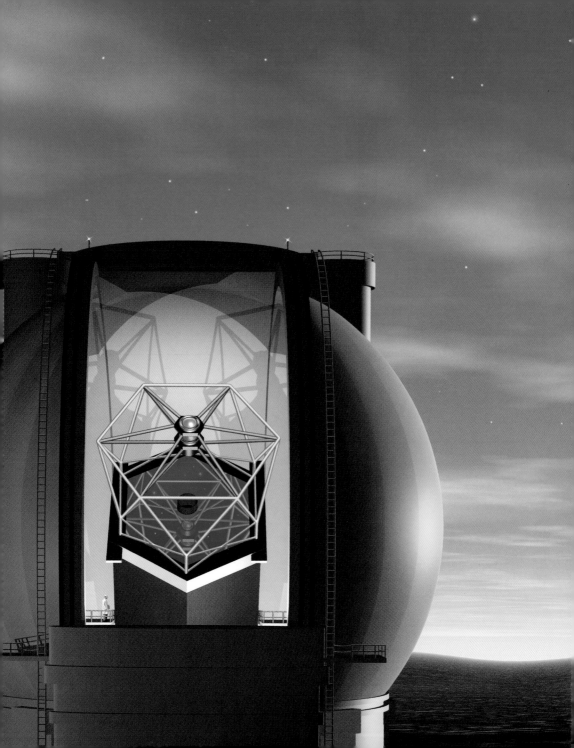

CHAPTER TWENTY
LOOKING AT THE NIGHT SKY

Who gazes at the stars?

We all enjoy looking up at the starry night sky, especially on a clear moonless night, away from bright city lights. Some people even star-gaze as a job. They are scientists called astronomers. Astronomy is the science of studying space and all the objects in it.

Astronomer and telescope

Amazing! You can see about 2,500 stars in the night sky! When the sky is clear, you can see that many different stars even without a telescope!

Studying a star chart

Can anyone be an astronomer?

Anyone can learn about stars as a hobby, but it takes years of study to do it as a job. You'll need books of star charts and maps, so you can recognize what you see. Binoculars or a telescope will let you see further.

Meteor shower

Is it true?
You can see the Moon's craters through binoculars.

Yes. Binoculars allow you to see the Moon's surface so clearly that you can make out individual craters – from 248,000 miles away!

Can you only see the Moon and stars at night?

The Moon and stars are easiest to spot, but even without a telescope you will see meteors (shooting stars) and the brighter planets, such as Venus, Jupiter or Mars. Venus shines white and is nicknamed the 'evening star'. Jupiter looks greeny-blue and Mars glows red.

Who first wrote about the stars?

The Babylonians were the first to write down their findings from studying the stars – around 5,000 years ago! They noticed that stars seem to form patterns, which we call constellations. The Babylonian empire was roughly where Iraq is today.

Babylonian astromomers

Is it true?

The Babylonians were maths wizards.

Yes. At first their findings about the night sky were based on looking and guessing. By around 500 BC, the Babylonians used sums to predict exactly when events such as eclipses would happen.

How do we know about the first astronomers?

The Babylonians didn't write on paper like we do. They wrote on clay tablets, so fragments have survived. Scientists called archaeologists dig in the ground for clues about ancient peoples such as the Babylonians.

Babylonian writing on a clay tablet

Amazing!

The Babylonians didn't see the same night sky as us. There were no twinkling satellites, and the stars were in different places because our Solar System has moved since then.

Clay tablet

What was a Babylonian year like?

The Babylonians worked out a 12-month year. Each month began with the first sight of the crescent Moon. The months were called Nisannu, Ayaru, Simanu, Du'uzu, Abu, Ululu, Tashritu, Arahsamnu, Kislimu, Tebetu, Shabatu and Addaru.

How did sailors know where they were going?

Out at sea, there are no landmarks. In the Middle Ages, sailors had special instruments that used the position of the Sun and stars to tell them where they were. These included compasses, astrolabes and cross-staffs.

Sailor and cross-staff

Amazing! The first astrolabes were made 1,500 years ago! Indian and Arab astronomers used pocket-sized instruments called astrolabes in the AD 500s.

No. You could use the position of the Sun instead of the stars, when you were sailing during the day. You looked at its position compared to the horizon.

What is the pole star?

The only star which doesn't appear to move is above the North Pole. Sailors could tell where they were by looking at the pole star – it's lowest in the sky at the Equator.

Path of the stars with the pole star in the middle

How did an astrolabe work?

An astrolabe had two discs, one with a star map, and the other with measuring lines and a pointer. You compared them with the Sun or a star and the horizon to work out your position.

Astrolabe

Who made the first telescope?

Hans Lippershey, a Dutch man who made spectacles, probably made the first telescope in 1608. He noticed that if he put two lenses at different ends of a tube and looked through them, objects seemed to be nearer and clearer.

Is it true?
Newton saw a rainbow in his telescope.

Yes. Isaac Newton noticed that the edges of objects seemed colored when you looked through a telescope. That's how he began to work out that clear white light is made up of many different colors.

Hans Lippershey with his telescope

 ## How does a telescope work?

The lens (curved piece of glass) at the front end of a telescope gathers light to make an image of an object that is far away. The lens at the back magnifies the image so it can be seen more clearly.

Simple cutaway of a telescope

Newton's reflecting telescope

Who put mirrors in a telescope?

Isaac Newton was the first person to make a mirror or reflecting telescope. He replaced the front lens with a dish-shaped mirror at the back. The mirror reflected the image on to a smaller mirror, and then into the eye.

Amazing! You can see Saturn's rings through a telescope. Telescopes magnify images (make them bigger) so much that you can even make out Saturn's faint rings – which are about 800 million miles away!

Nicolaus
Copernicus

Who said that planets go round the Sun?

Nicolaus Copernicus explained this idea in a book in 1543. The problem was, the Church stated that God had put the Earth at the center of the Universe. You could be put to death for saying that the Earth went round the Sun.

Who was put on trial for star-gazing?

Few scientists were brave enough to say that they agreed with Copernicus's findings that the Earth went round the Sun. The Italian astronomer Galileo was – and was put on trial for his ideas in 1634.

Is it true?

The Church accepted that Galileo was right in the end.

Yes. The Church eventually agreed that the Earth and other planets traveled round the Sun. But they didn't do this until 1992 – 350 years after Galileo's death!

Galileo on trial

Who first used a telescope for astronomy?

Galileo started making telescopes in 1609, not long after Lippershey made his. Galileo was the first person to realize how useful a telescope would be for looking at the night sky. Because he could see more clearly, he made lots of important new finds, such as discovering four of Jupiter's moons.

 Amazing! Copernicus explained the seasons. By showing that the Earth goes round the Sun and also spins at the same time, Copernicus explained why some times of the year are warmer than others.

Galileo looking at the night sky

Where do astronomers put their telescopes?

Observatories are buildings where astronomers go to look at the sky. They house the most powerful telescopes on Earth. The telescopes are usually kept in a room with a dome-shaped roof. Observatories have other instruments too, such as very precise clocks, to help keep accurate time and records.

Pulkovo Observatory, Russia

Mount Cerro
Observatory, Chile

Where's the best place to build an observatory?

Where you'll get the clearest view! Most are built away from city lights. Mountain-tops are best of all, because they poke above any clouds that might spoil the view.

Is it true?
The Greenwich Observatory
houses the most telescopes.

No. The Kitt Peak National Observatory
in Arizona, USA has the most optical
telescopes. One of them, the Mayall
Telescope, is 13 feet across!

Amazing! The
Ancient
Babylonians used
observatories. They did their
star-gazing from stepped
towers called ziggurats.

Telescope in a domed
observatory

How can a telescope see through the roof?

It doesn't have to – an
observatory's domed
roof is specially
designed to slide open
at night, so that the
picture through the
telescope isn't
distorted (blurred) by
looking through a
window. The telescope
can be pointed at any
place in the sky.

How deep is space?

Early astronomers thought that all the stars were the same distance from us, forming a simple shell around the Earth. Now we know that some stars are relatively close to us, and others are trillions of miles away.

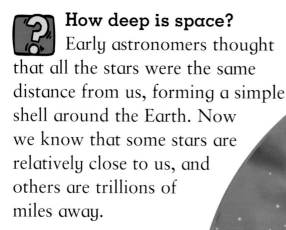

Gaseous clouds in deep space

Is it true?

We measure how far the stars are in miles.

No. They're so far away, that we use light years instead. A light year is how far light travels in one year – 5866 billion miles!

NEAREST STAR
25 000 000 000 000 miles

Are there candles in space?

Not really. But we can see how far away a galaxy is by the brightness of a special type of star, called a 'standard candle'. The further away the galaxy, the dimmer the candle.

How do you measure the distance to a star?

Watch the tip of your finger as you move it towards to your nose. The closer it gets, the more cross-eyed you become! Astronomers can tell the distance to a star by measuring how 'cross-eyed' a pair of telescopes has to be to see it.

 Amazing! Galaxies move so quickly they are different colors. The light waves from them change, just as a fire trucks siren sounds lower after it zooms past. We use the color to measure the galaxies' speed.

Who made the first radio telescope?

Radio telescopes are like giant satellite dishes that pick up invisible radio waves and similar waves, instead of light rays. Unlike light, radio waves can travel through cloud, so radio telescopes can be built just about anywhere! An American called Grote Reber made the first one in the 1930s.

Reber's radio telescope was a simple metal frame.

Amazing! A telescope can be 5,000 miles long. The Very Long Baseline Array (VLBA) stretches across the USA. It has ten different dishes and produces the best-quality radio images of space from Earth yet!

Which are the most powerful radio telescopes?

The ones that are made up of several different radio dishes, such as the Very Large Array (VLA) in New Mexico, USA. The VLA has 27 dishes, each 82 feet across. Scientists compare the findings from all 27 dishes to get super-accurate results.

VLA, Socorro, New Mexico

Where is the biggest radio telescope?

The world's biggest single-dish radio telescope was built in Puerto Rico in the Caribbean about 40 years ago. It is 985 feet across – so it would take you more than ten minutes to walk around the edge of it.

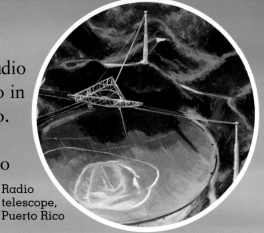

Radio telescope, Puerto Rico

 ### Is it true?
Only ten astronomers are allowed to use the VLA.

No. It is used by over 500 astronomers a year. Some study our near-neighbors in the Solar System, while others peer way beyond our galaxy to others in deepest space.

What's better than a powerful telescope?
Seeing for yourself in close-up – but it's too
dangerous and expensive to send astronomers
deep into space. That's why space probes are
such important tools. Space probes are fitted
with cameras. They beam back close-up
photos of faraway planets and comets.

Amazing! Chandra is a
billion times more powerful
than the first X-ray telescope.
If telescopes keep improving at this
rate, we'll be able to see the farthest
edges of the Universe in 30 years' time!

Cassini-
Huygens
spacecraft

Is it true?
A probe found a watery world.

Yes. The Voyager 2 probe photographed what might be water on Jupiter's moon, Europa. If there is life out there, probes will probably find it first.

Could we build Very Large Arrays in space?
Scientists are already testing a cluster of satellites that fly in perfect formation, using laser beams. The same technology will be used to create a string of small satellite telescopes, making one huge 'eye' in space.

VLA in space

Moon observatory of the future

Could we build an observatory on the Moon?
The dark side of the Moon would be a perfect site. Always pointing away from the Earth, it is shielded from man-made X-rays. But building there would be very expensive.

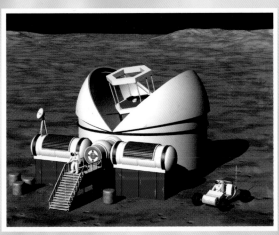

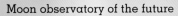

419

CHAPTER TWENTY ONE
PREHISTORIC LIFE
ON EARTH

How old is the Earth?

Earth is millions and millions of years old. In fact, our planet is four-thousand-six-hundred-million years old. When the Earth's age (4.6 billion years) is written as a number, it looks like this: 4,600,000,000. It's hard for us to imagine anything so old.

Earth today

Fiery conditions on Earth before life began

 Amazing! Some of Earth's oldest known rocks are found in Scotland. They are about 3.5 billion years old.

 ## Has there always been life on the Earth?

Nothing at all lived on the Earth for the first billion (1,000 million) years of the planet's existence. The conditions were not right for life. There were no plants or animals of any kind. Earth was a dangerous place where life could not survive.

200 million years ago

150 million years ago

80 million years ago

 Has the Earth always looked the same?

These maps show how Earth's land and sea looked in the past. To fit everything on them, Earth has been drawn as an oval. For a long time, all land was joined together in one giant mass. Over millions of years it broke up into smaller pieces. They turned into today's continents.

 Is it true?
The continents are still moving.

Yes. The continents move about one and a half inches each year – the length of your little finger. Millions of years in the future, Earth will look very different from today.

When and where did life on Earth begin?

Life on Earth began about 3.5 billion years ago. The first life appeared in the sea. It was born into a world that looked very different from today. The atmosphere was filled with poisonous gases. The sky was pink, and the sea was rusty-red.

Conditions on Earth were hostile when life first began.

Is it true?
Earth is the only planet with life on it.

Maybe. This is one of the greatest unsolved mysteries. Life probably does exist on other planets besides Earth, but nothing has been found so far. The search continues.

Beginnings of life

How did life begin?

It is thought that life began when lightning hit the sea. Lightning sent energy into the water. Chemicals in the sea were mixed together by energy. New substances, called amino acids, were made, from which life was able to grow.

Amazing!
The first living things on Earth were so small you could fit thousands of them on the head of a pin.

What were the first living things?

The first living things were bacteria. They lived in the sea. Some bacteria changed into algae, which were simple plants. Algae lived in the sea in masses, like huge blankets. They made oxygen, which helped to turn the sky and sea blue.

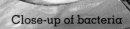

Close-up of bacteria

425

When did life first appear on land?

About 440 million years ago, the first life appeared on land. It was simple plant life, similar to today's mosses. Then, about 400 million years ago, the first land animals – worms, spiders, scorpions and insects – evolved as they moved on to the land.

Is it true?
There are no amphibians alive today.

No. There are many different amphibians in the world today. Frogs, toads and salamanders are all amphibians.

Scorpion

Cockroach

Centipede

Why did some fish grow legs?

Some fish began to live in shallow water. It was difficult to swim in the shallows. To help these fish move around they grew short legs. Some of them also grew lungs, which meant they could breathe air. These animals could live in water and on land.

Acanthostega (an early amphibian)

Amazing! The lungfish is one of today's fish that can live out of water. It can breathe air.

Which animal lives in water and on land?

An animal that can live in water and on land is called an amphibian. It means 'double life'. The first amphibians appeared by 350 million years ago. Gradually, they spent more and more time on land.

Ichthyostega
(an early amphibian)

What are reptiles?

About 300 million years ago, some amphibians changed into reptiles. They could live on land all the time. Reptiles have backbones and scaly skin, and most lay eggs. Many reptiles, such as crocodiles, spend lots of time in the water, but they can't breathe underwater. They use the Sun to keep their bodies warm.

Is it true?

Some early reptiles had sails, on their backs.

Yes. Dimetrodon had a skin 'sail' on its back. It soaked up the Sun's heat, and controlled the animal's body temperature.

Hylonomus

What did reptiles eat?

The first reptiles, such as Hylonomus, were small lizard-like animals that ate tiny creatures. Reptiles learned how to run quickly so they could catch fast-moving insects. As reptiles became larger, they caught and ate bigger prey, including other reptiles. Some reptiles only ate plants.

Amazing! A small animal found in Scotland, in rocks that are 350 million years old, might be one of the first reptiles. But some scientists say it was an amphibian.

Hylonomus and dragonfly

Which reptiles had fur?

Some prehistoric reptiles grew fur on their bodies to keep themselves warm. These were the cynodonts. They lived about 245 million years ago. Over time they changed into a completely new group of animals, called mammals.

Cynognathus (a cynodont)

Thrinaxodon (a cynodont)

What are birds?

Birds are animals with backbones, they lay eggs, can make their own body heat, and have wings. They are also the only animals with feathers. Not all birds can fly. The first birds lived at the same time as the dinosaurs.

Phororhacos

Prophaeton

Is it true?
Ostrich eggs are the biggest eggs ever laid by a bird.

No. The extinct bird Aepyornis laid the biggest eggs of all time. Each one was about the size of 150 hen's eggs.

Hyracotherium (a very small, early kind of horse)

Where do birds come from?

Birds evolved from small, meat-eating dinosaurs. Fossils show that some of these dinosaurs had feathers. They are called 'dinobirds'. The first 'dinobirds' probably could not fly.

Caudipteryx

Fossilised Archaeopteryx

Amazing! Today's hoatzin bird, which lives in South America, has claws on its wings when young – just like Archaeopteryx, its prehistoric ancestor did.

Archaeopteryx

Which was the first true bird?

The first true bird – a bird that could fly – appeared about 150 million years ago. It is known as Archaeopteryx, which means 'ancient wing'. It had claws on its wings.

What are mammals?

Mammals have backbones, their bodies are covered in hair or bristles, they make their own body heat, and they feed their young on milk. They have larger brains than most other animals.

Early mammals

Ginkgo tree

When did the first mammals appear?

The first mammals appeared on Earth about 220 million years ago. They lived at the same time as the dinosaurs. Mammals survived after the dinosaurs died out, and then they became the ruling animals on Earth. There are about 4,200 different kinds of mammals alive today.

Amazing! Woolly mammoths were big elephants with extra-long tusks up to 10 feet long. Their bodies were covered in fur.

Did mammals only live on land?

Mammals came to live in all of Earth's habitats. Many lived on land, but some, such as bats, were able to glide through the air on wings of skin. Other mammals swam in the sea, such as whales, dolphins and seals.

Basilosaurus

Tyrannosaurus rex

Is it true?
The elephant is the largest land mammal ever to have lived.

No. Indricotherium was the largest land mammal. It was almost 26 feet tall and as heavy as four elephants.

Megazostrodon

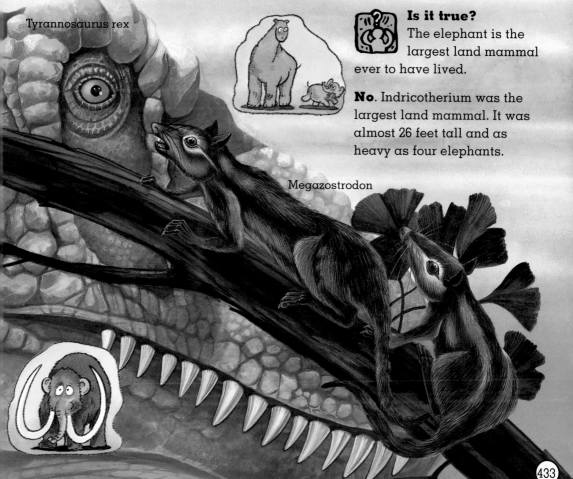

Homo
habilis

Homo
erectus

Who were the very first humans?

The first people we think of as humans appeared in Africa. About two million years ago, Homo habilis (handy man) appeared. Then, more than one million years ago, Homo erectus (upright man) appeared, but they weren't modern humans.

Hand axe

Fire-making tool

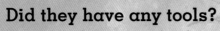

Flint knife

Did they have any tools?

Homo habilis was the first tool-user. This is why he is called 'handy man'. He made simple tools, such as choppers, from pebbles. The tools made by Homo erectus were better. He shaped stones into hand axes, and he was the first to use fire.

What did they eat?

Homo habilis and Homo erectus ate meat and plants. Meat probably came from dead animals which they found. They may have hunted for some small animals. Plants gave them berries and leaves. They used stone tools to cut and scrape their food.

Is it true?
Homo erectus was a wanderer.

Yes. More than one million years ago, Homo erectus began to move out of Africa, traveling to Europe and Asia.

Homo erectus people hunted and gathered their food.

Amazing! Homo erectus had fire. Fire provided warmth, gave heat for cooking, and offered protection from predators.

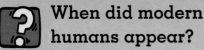
When did modern humans appear?

Just over 100,000 years ago Homo sapiens appeared. The name means 'wise man'. They were modern humans. In Europe they lived during the freezing Ice Age, a time when glaciers covered the land. The Ice Age ended 12,000 years ago.

Mammoth hunt

Is it true?

Homo sapiens have all died out.

No. All people on Earth today are members of Homo sapiens. If they had died out, like other kinds of early human, none of us would be here today!

Where did they live?

Homo sapiens first appeared in Africa, and from there, they spread out across the world. They lived in cave entrances, and in places sheltered by overhanging rocks. In the open they made huts from branches, covered with skins.

As the climate grew warmer, Homo sapiens people migrated across the world.

Amazing! People who lived during the Ice Age played musical instruments. They made whistles from bones, and drums from shoulder-blades.

Animal carving

Cave painting

Were they artists?

The humans who lived in Europe during the Ice Age were among the first artists. They painted pictures of horses, bison and deer on the walls of their caves. Bone and ivory were carved into figures of animals and people.

437

How do we know about life in the past?

We find out about life in the past by looking for evidence. Fossils are one kind of evidence. They are the remains of living things that have been preserved. Objects made by humans, such as stone tools, are another kind of evidence.

A collection of fossils

Is it true?
Plants can't be fossilized.

No. Plants can become fossils, in the same way that animals can. By studying them we learn about the plants that once grew on Earth.

1

2

3

4

How is a fossil made?

It takes millions of years to make a fossil. The pictures on the left show how it happens. (1) An animal dies. Its body sinks to the bottom of a lake. (2) Sand and silt cover its body. (3) The flesh rots away. Minerals seep into the bones and turn them to stone. The animal is now a fossil. (4) The fossil is found.

Who looks for prehistoric life?

People who look for remains of prehistoric animals, such as dinosaurs, are called paleontologists. People who look for ancient humans are archaeologists. They find great things, such as bones, tools, buildings, jewelry and weapons.

Paleontologists excavating fossilized dinosaur bones

Amazing! A sticky resin that oozed from pine trees trapped insects that landed on it. It hardened into a substance called amber. Prehistoric insects are perfectly preserved inside it.

439

CHAPTER TWENTY TWO
EXPLORING EARTH

Earth

24,847 miles

How big is the Earth?

The Earth is shaped like a gigantic ball, slightly squashed at the top and bottom. Around its middle, where it's fattest, it measures 24,847 miles. It would take you almost a year to walk right round the Earth, without a rest.

Inner mantle

Core

Interior of Earth

What's inside the Earth?

The Earth is made up of layers of rock and metal. We live on the hard, rocky surface, called the crust. Below, the layers are so hot that they've melted and turned runny. The center of the Earth is a ball of almost solid metal.

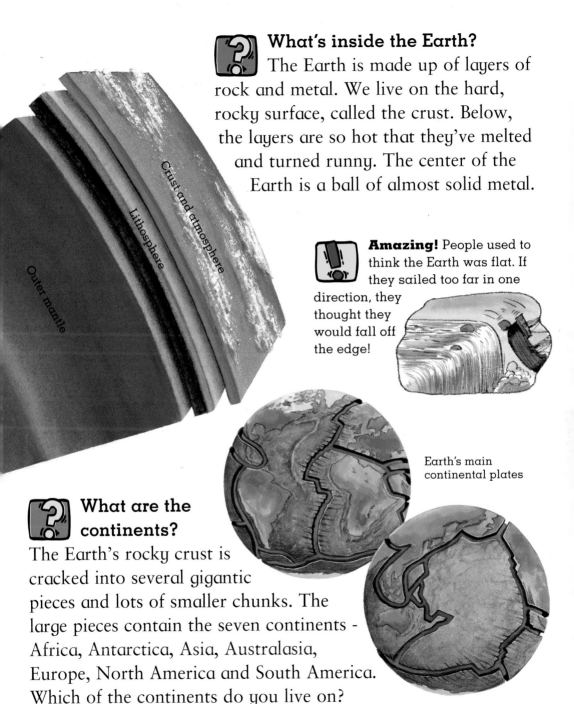

Crust and atmosphere

Lithosphere

Outer mantle

Amazing! People used to think the Earth was flat. If they sailed too far in one direction, they thought they would fall off the edge!

Earth's main continental plates

What are the continents?

The Earth's rocky crust is cracked into several gigantic pieces and lots of smaller chunks. The large pieces contain the seven continents - Africa, Antarctica, Asia, Australasia, Europe, North America and South America. Which of the continents do you live on?

Where are the Poles?

The North and South Poles are at either end of the Earth. The North Pole is surrounded by the frozen Arctic Ocean. The South Pole is in the middle of icy Antarctica.

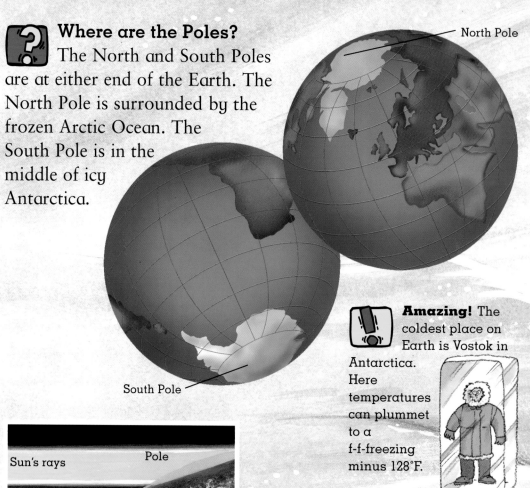

North Pole

South Pole

Amazing! The coldest place on Earth is Vostok in Antarctica. Here temperatures can plummet to a f-f-freezing minus 128°F.

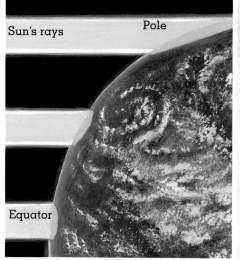

Sun's rays

Pole

Equator

Why are the Poles cold?

The Poles are the coldest places on Earth. They're battered by blizzards and covered in ice and snow. The Poles are cold because the Sun's rays hit them at a slant, so they're spread out and very weak.

Is it true?
Penguins live at the
North Pole.

No. Penguins only live around
the South Pole. But you might
bump into a polar bear at the
North Pole.

 ## Who reached the South Pole first?

The first person to reach the
South Pole was Norwegian
explorer Roald Amundsen in
December 1911. He beat the
British team of Captain Scott
by about a month. Exhausted
and suffering from frostbite,
Scott died on the way home.

Captain Scott in the Antarctic

Amazing! In 1912, the luxury liner, Titanic, hit an iceberg and sank in the North Atlantic. It was on its maiden (first) voyage from Southampton to New York.

Iceberg seen from underwater

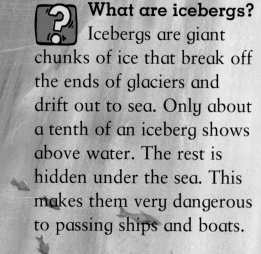

 What are icebergs?
Icebergs are giant chunks of ice that break off the ends of glaciers and drift out to sea. Only about a tenth of an iceberg shows above water. The rest is hidden under the sea. This makes them very dangerous to passing ships and boats.

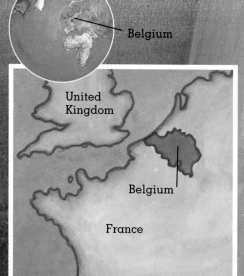

Belgium

United Kingdom

Belgium

France

Which was the biggest iceberg?
The biggest iceberg ever was seen near Antarctica. It was about the size of Belgium! The tallest iceberg was more than half as high as the Eiffel Tower in Paris.

Is it true?
Baby icebergs are
called calves.

Yes. When a baby iceberg
breaks off a glacier, it is called
'calving'. Even smaller
icebergs are called 'bergy bits'.

 **Which is the longest
glacier?**

Glaciers are enormous rivers
of ice that flow slowly down
a mountainside.
The Lambert-Fisher Glacier
in Antarctica is over 370
miles long. It's the longest
glacier in the world. About a
tenth of the Earth is covered
in icy glaciers.

Glacier

Why does the sea flow in and out?

Twice a day, the sea washes on to the shore at high tide. Then it flows back out again at low tide. The tides are caused by the Moon and Sun pulling the sea into giant bulges on either side of the Earth.

 Amazing! If all the coasts were straightened out, they'd stretch round the Earth 13 times. At 55,800 miles, Canada has the longest coast.

Cliffs being worn down to make sand

Why are beaches sandy?

Sand is made from tiny fragments of rock and shells, crushed up by the wind and water. Sand is usually yellow or white. But some sand is black because it contains volcanic rock or coal.

Sandy beach

How are cliffs carved out?

Along the coast, the rocks are worn away by the force of the waves. As the waves crash against the shore, they carve out cliffs, caves and high arches. Sometimes an arch collapses, leaving a stack, or pillar, of rock.

Features of chalk cliffs

Stack

Arch

Headland

Is it true?
White horses swim in the sea.

Yes. But they're not real horses. They're the white, foamy tops of the waves as they gallop towards the shore.

? How big is the sea?

The sea is absolutely huge! Salty sea water covers about two-thirds of our planet so there's far more sea than land. The sea lies in five oceans – the Pacific, Atlantic, Indian, Arctic and Southern Oceans.

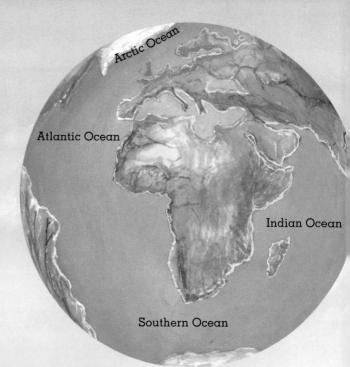

Arctic Ocean

Atlantic Ocean

Indian Ocean

Southern Ocean

Amazing! The first person to set sail around the world was Ferdinand Magellan. He set off from Spain in 1519. Magellan died but one of his ships made it back three years later.

Malaysia

Pacific Ocean

Panama

Southern Ocean

Which is the biggest ocean?

By far the biggest ocean is the vast Pacific. It alone covers a third of the Earth. At its widest point, between Panama and Malaysia, it stretches almost halfway around the world.

Is it true?
The Arctic is the warmest ocean.

No. The Arctic's the coldest ocean of all. For most of the year, it's covered in ice.

Why is the sea salty?

The sea's salty taste comes from ordinary salt. It's the same stuff you sprinkle on your food. The rain washes the salt out of rocks on land, then rivers carry it into the sea. The people in the picture are collecting salt left after sea water dries.

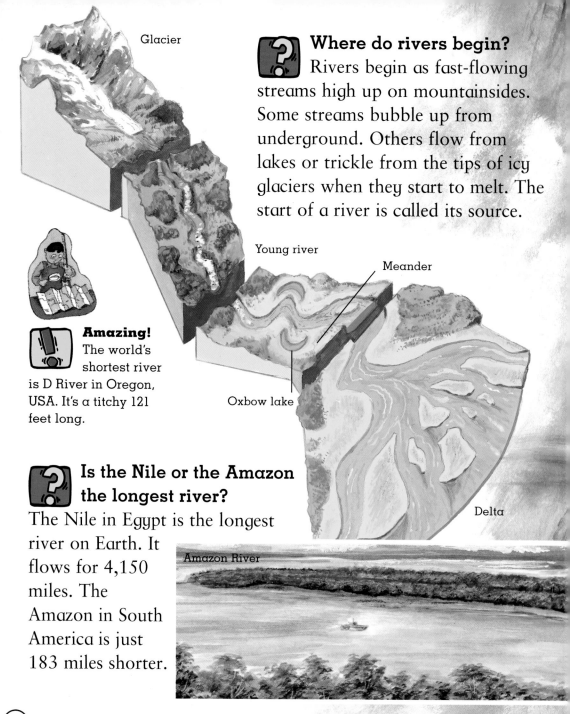

Glacier

Young river

Meander

Oxbow lake

Delta

Amazon River

Where do rivers begin?

Rivers begin as fast-flowing streams high up on mountainsides. Some streams bubble up from underground. Others flow from lakes or trickle from the tips of icy glaciers when they start to melt. The start of a river is called its source.

Amazing! The world's shortest river is D River in Oregon, USA. It's a titchy 121 feet long.

Is the Nile or the Amazon the longest river?

The Nile in Egypt is the longest river on Earth. It flows for 4,150 miles. The Amazon in South America is just 183 miles shorter.

Angel Falls

How high are waterfalls?

The highest waterfall in the world is Angel Falls in Venezuela. It plunges 3,212 feet down the side of a mountain. Angel Falls are 20 times higher than the famous Niagara Falls in North America.

Is it true?
Rivers flow into the sea.

Yes. Most rivers flow into the sea at their deltas. But some rivers flow into lakes and a few flow into deserts.

Which lake is the biggest?

The biggest freshwater lake on Earth is Lake Superior in North America. It covers 51,000 square miles. That's almost as big as Austria. Lake Superior is one of five huge lakes called the Great Lakes.

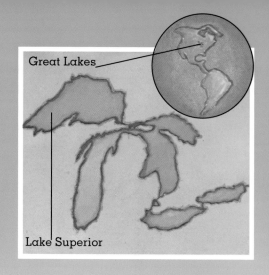

Great Lakes

Lake Superior

Amazing! The Dead Sea in the Middle East is so salty, you can float on the surface. No fish can live in it.

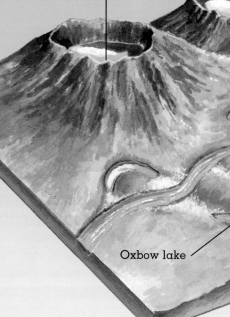

Volcanic lake

Oxbow lake

Is it true? There's a monster in Loch Ness.

Maybe. Some people say Nessie is a type of prehistoric reptile that lives in the lake. Others say this is nonsense. What do you think?

Lake
Titicaca

Where is the highest lake?

Lake Titicaca in South America is the highest lake on which boats can sail. It's 12,500 feet up in the Andes Mountains. People who live around the lake build boats from lake reeds.

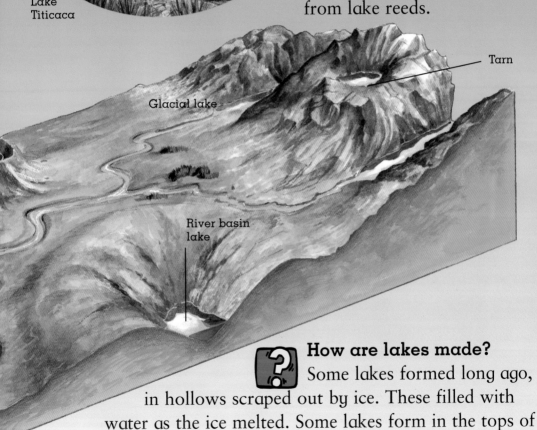

Tarn

Glacial lake

River basin lake

How are lakes made?

Some lakes formed long ago, in hollows scraped out by ice. These filled with water as the ice melted. Some lakes form in the tops of volcanoes or when a river cuts through a bend.

Why are deserts dry?

Deserts are the driest places on Earth. In some deserts it doesn't rain for years at a time. In others, it never rains at all. Some deserts are also scorching hot. In the daytime, the sand's hot enough to fry an egg on.

Amazing! The Sahara Desert is the biggest, sandiest desert in the world. It covers about a third of Africa.

Sandy desert seen from above

Can sand dunes move?

Strong winds blowing across the desert pile the sand up into giant heaps, or dunes. The biggest stand 650 feet tall. The dunes creep forward every year and can bury whole desert villages.

Sand dunes covering a town

Mesa

Butte

Sand dunes

Salt lake

Dried salt flat

Rocky desert

Volcanic desert

Desert landscapes

Are all deserts sandy?
No, they're not. Only about a quarter of all deserts are sandy. Most deserts are rocky or covered in gravel and stones. Some deserts have high mountains or strange-shaped rocks towering up from the ground.

Is it true?
Mushrooms grow in the desert.

Yes. Well, mushroom-shaped rocks. They're carved into shape by sand blown by the wind, like a giant piece of sandpaper.

? Why are rainforests so wet?

Because it rains almost every single day! Late most afternoons, the sky goes black and there's a heavy thunderstorm. Rainforests grow along the equator where it's hot and sticky all year round. It's the perfect weather for plants to grow.

Coniferous forest

Rainforest

Where do the biggest forests grow?

 The biggest forests in the world stretch for thousands of miles across the north of Europe and Asia. The trees that grow here are conifers. They're trees with needle-like leaves and cones.

Is it true?
The paper we use comes from forests.

Yes. You could make more than 1,500 copies of this book from a single conifer tree.

 **Amazing!** The biggest rainforest grows in South America along the banks of the River Amazon. It's home to millions of plants and animals.

Emergent layer

Canopy layer

Understorey

Ground layer

Rainforest layers

How do rainforests grow?

Rainforests grow in layers depending on the height of the trees. The tallest trees poke out above the forest. Below them is a thick roof of tree-tops called the canopy. Next comes a layer of shorter trees, herbs and shrubs.

African savannah (grassland)

What are grasslands?

Grasslands are huge plains of grass, trees and bushes. They grow in warm, dry places where there's too little rain for forests to grow, but enough rain to stop the land turning into a desert.

South American gauchos farming on grassland

 ## Why did a grassland turn to dust?

In the 1930s, farmers in the south-west USA ploughed up the grasslands to grow wheat. But a terrible drought turned the soil to dry, useless dust which blew away in the wind. This was called a dustbowl.

Amazing! Grassland animals eat different bits of the grass to avoid competition – zebras eat the tops, wildebeest eat the stems.

Dustbowl

What are grasslands used for?

People use grasslands for grazing animals such as cattle which are raised for their meat. They also grow crops such as wheat and barley in gigantic fields. One wheat field in Canada was the size of 20,000 soccer pitches.

Is it true? Rice is a type of grass.

Yes. Rice is a cereal plant, which belongs to the grass family. The grains of rice come from the flower-heads. Rice grows in flooded fields in South East Asia.

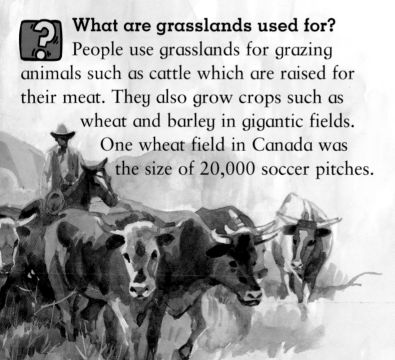

CHAPTER TWENTY THREE
VIOLENT EARTH

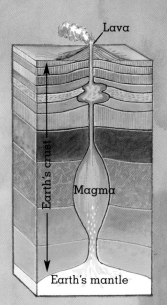

Lava

Earth's crust

Magma

Earth's mantle

 Why do volcanoes blow their tops?

Volcanoes are mountains that spit fire. Deep under the Earth there is red-hot, runny rock called magma. Sometimes the magma bursts up through a crack in the Earth's crust and a volcano erupts.

 Amazing! Some of the world's highest mountains are volcanoes. They include Mt Kilimanjaro in Africa. Luckily for this nosy lion, Kilimanjaro is now long extinct.

Pompeii, AD 79

Volcano erupting

What is lava?

Once magma has erupted from a volcano, it is called lava. Some lava is thick and lumpy. Some is thin and runny. In the air, it cools and turns into hard, black rock.

Is it true?

Volcanic ash can flow as fast as a train.

Yes. Clouds of gas and ash can flow across the ground at over 100 mph!

What happened to Pompeii?

In AD 79, Mt Vesuvius in Italy blew its top in a massive explosion. The nearby city of Pompeii was buried under a huge cloud of hot ash and rock. Thousands of people were suffocated. Others fled for their lives.

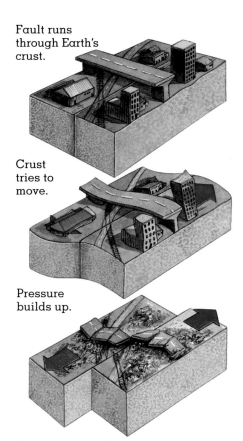

Fault runs through Earth's crust.

Crust tries to move.

Pressure builds up.

Earthquake finally occurs as pieces move apart with a jerk.

 ## What makes the Earth shake?

The Earth's surface is cracked into enormous pieces which drift on the red-hot, runny rock below. Sometimes two pieces push and shove each other, making the Earth shake.

Kobe earthquake, Japan, 1995

How much damage do earthquakes cause?

Big earthquakes do lots of damage. Huge cracks open up in the ground. Houses, roads and bridges shake and fall down. In the worst earthquakes, many people are killed and injured by buildings that collapse on them.

How do scientists measure an earthquake?

An earthquake sends shock waves rippling through the ground. Scientists study these waves to see how big the earthquake is. They measure earthquakes on a scale of 1 to 10. Each quake on the scale is 30 times worse than the one before.

Seismograph (earthquake measuring device)

Is it true?
People used to think earthquakes were caused by fish.

Yes. In Japan, people thought quakes were caused by a giant catfish wriggling about on the sea bed. The gods had to put a rock on the fish's head to make it stay still!

How do floods happen?

Many floods happen when it rains very heavily and rivers overflow. They burst their banks and flood the land all around. You also get floods in stormy weather when high tides or gigantic waves sweep on to the shore.

Flash flood of
Ouvèze River, France

Amazing! The Thames Barrier was finished in 1984 to stop the River Thames flooding and drowning London. Ten huge steel gates swing up to make a massive dam.

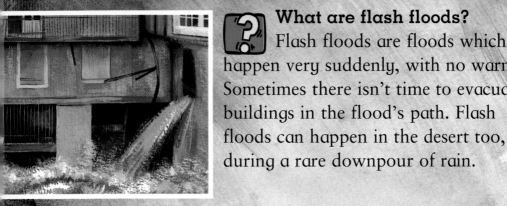

What are flash floods?

Flash floods are floods which happen very suddenly, with no warning. Sometimes there isn't time to evacuate buildings in the flood's path. Flash floods can happen in the desert too, during a rare downpour of rain.

Is it true?
Floods can wash whole buildings away.

Yes. In 1955, a flood in the USA washed a four-story wooden hotel clean away. Imagine how surprised the guests were when they looked out of their windows!

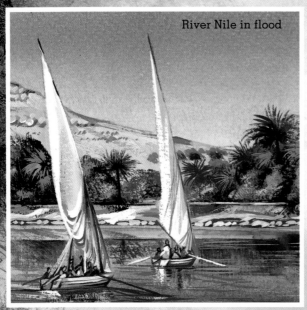

River Nile in flood

Are some floods useful?

Yes, they are. The River Nile in Egypt used to flood every year, leaving rich mud on the fields. The mud made the soil ideal for farmers to grow bumper crops. The Nile doesn't flood any more because a large dam was built to store its water.

The Mississippi River, USA, flooded 50,000 square miles, in 1993.

When do thunderstorms happen?

Thunderstorms usually happen on a hot, summer's day when the air is warm and sticky. Watch out for huge, dark, tall thunderclouds gathering in the sky. They're a sure sign a storm's brewing. Time to head indoors!

What makes thunder rumble?

Lightning is incredibly hot, about five times hotter than the Sun's surface. As it streaks through the sky, it heats the air so quickly that it makes a loud booming sound. This is the sound of thunder.

Where do thunderstorms begin?

Thunder starts in cumulonimbus clouds. They turn the sky purply black and blue. Some of these clouds are massive. The tallest can grow 11 miles high. That's more than twice the height of Mt Everest.

Cumulonimbus thundercloud

Is it true?
Lightning happens before thunder.

No. They happen at exactly the same time. But you see lightning before you hear thunder because light travels more quickly than sound.

Amazing! The Vikings believed that thunder was caused by the bad-tempered god, Thor, hurling his hammer across the sky.

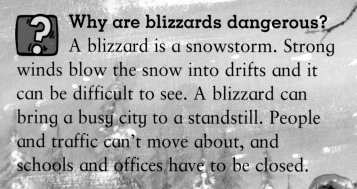

Why are blizzards dangerous?

A blizzard is a snowstorm. Strong winds blow the snow into drifts and it can be difficult to see. A blizzard can bring a busy city to a standstill. People and traffic can't move about, and schools and offices have to be closed.

Amazing! You don't only get snow in cold places. In 1981, snow fell in the Kalahari Desert in Africa for the first time in living memory. The temperature dropped to a chilly 23°F.

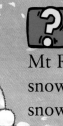

Which is the snowiest place?

The snowiest place in the world is Mt Rainier in Washington, USA. In one year, snow 100 feet deep fell there. That's enough snow to build a snowman as tall as 17 people. Fancy having a go?

Build-up of a hailstone within a thundercloud

What is a hailstone made from?

A hailstone is a small ball of ice that starts life in a thundercloud. Inside the cloud, a chip of ice is tossed up and down many times. It gets coated in layers of ice, just like the layers of an onion.

Cutaway of a hailstone, showing the layers of ice

Record-breaking hailstone

 Is it true?
The biggest hailstone was the size of a peach.

No. It was bigger than that! Hailstones are usually the size of peas but the biggest was the size of a watermelon. It fell in Kansas, USA, in 1970.

473

What are hurricanes?

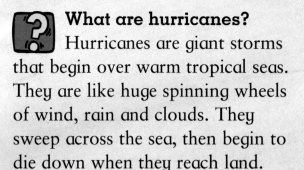

Hurricanes are giant storms that begin over warm tropical seas. They are like huge spinning wheels of wind, rain and clouds. They sweep across the sea, then begin to die down when they reach land.

An Atlantic hurricane hits the island of Antigua.

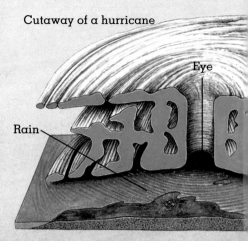

Cutaway of a hurricane

Eye

Rain

Is it true?

Hurricanes have names.

Yes. Hurricanes are given names from an alphabetical list. A new list is made every year. The names of the worst hurricanes, like Andrew or Carol, are never used again.

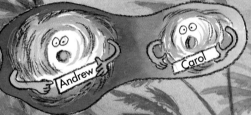

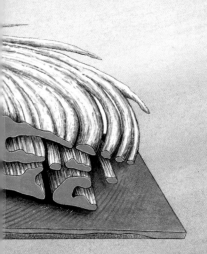

How big are hurricanes?

 Hurricanes can be enormous. Some measure 1,800 miles across and even the smallest are about half the size of Britain. Winds inside a hurricane can blow at over 180 mph.

 Amazing! If you could collect the energy inside a hurricane for one day and turn it into electricity, it would run the whole USA for six months.

Hurricanes can even pick up and dump airplanes.

Do hurricanes have eyes?

 Yes, they do. The eye is a patch of calm, clear weather in the hurricane's center. As the eye passes over land, there's a break in the storm for an hour or so. Then it begins again.

Eye of hurricane seen from space

What makes a tornado twist?

A tornado is a fierce, twisting wind which hangs from a thundercloud. It starts when wind inside the cloud starts to spin very quickly. A twisty tornado speeds across the ground, sucking up everything in its way.

Storm chasers observing a tornado in Kansas, USA

Amazing! Some people track tornadoes for fun. They drive as close to the twister as they dare, then take video films and photographs. It's a very dangerous hobby!

A tornado leaving a trail of damage

Is it true?
Tornadoes can pick up trains.

Yes. In 1931, a tornado in Minnesota, USA, picked a train right off its tracks and dumped it in a ditch. Tornadoes often pick up cars and cows!

How quickly do tornadoes travel?

Most tornadoes travel at about 18 mph, but some are much speedier movers. They race along the ground as quickly as a car. What's more, the wind inside a tornado can blow at an amazing 300 mph.

Do tornadoes happen at sea?

Yes, they're called waterspouts. These giant twists of water can be a mile tall. In the past, sailors thought waterspouts were sea monsters!

Waterspouts suck up tons of water from the sea.

Firefighting plane

How do wildfires start?

They destroy huge patches of forest, and spread very quickly, especially in dry weather. Lightning starts hundreds of wildfires a year. But most fires are started by people to clear space for farms and fields. These fires can quickly get out of control.

Is it true?

Some trees have fireproof bark.

Yes. Many trees die in forest fires because their wood easily catches fire. But some trees have special bark which protects the wood inside from the flames.

 ## How do people fight wildfires?

Fighting a wildfire is difficult and dangerous. Special planes fly overhead spraying the forest with millions of gallons of water. Firefighters on the ground try to hold back the fire with water and beaters.

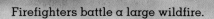
Firefighters battle a large wildfire.

What is a heatwave?

A heatwave is very hot weather which lasts much longer than usual. The scorching heat can kill people, animals and crops. It also dries up reservoirs, and melts the surface of roads.

Duststorm during the Midwest USA heatwave, 1937

 Amazing! It can take hundreds of years for a forest to grow again after a fire. But sometimes fires can be good for forests. They clear space for new plants to grow.

El Niño is represented by the red areas along the center of the Earth.

What is El Niño?

El Niño is a warm band of water which flows in the sea along the coast of South America. Scientists blame El Niño for changing the weather, by causing more storms, floods, droughts and tornadoes every few years.

Is it true?

It can rain cats and dogs.

No. But you can get showers of fish, frogs, flowers, coal, nuts and even maggots! Scientists think the wind scoops them up, then they fall again in the rain.

What are monsoons?

Monsoons are winds which bring heavy rain to tropical places such as India and South East Asia, during the summer months. Farmers rely on this rain to water their crops, because during the cooler months, there might be little or no rainfall.

Amazing! A turtle once fell in a hailstone in the USA. It had somehow been sucked up into a thundercloud and covered in layers of ice.

The monsoon season can bring severe flooding.

What is a sandstorm?

A sandstorm is a thick, choking cloud of sand whipped up by the wind in the desert. If you get caught in a sandstorm the best thing to do is cover your nose and mouth. Then you won't breathe the choking sand in.

Sandstorm in Africa

CHAPTER TWENTY FOUR
OUR EARTH

Is Earth a healthy planet?

Look at Earth from space and you see a mainly blue, watery planet with swirling white clouds. All looks well, but get closer, and you see a different picture. Parts of Earth are unhealthy – and all because of the way we live.

Earth seen from space

Does Earth need looking after?

Earth is our only home – we can't live on other planets. We need to look after it to make sure it stays a beautiful, healthy place. If we don't care for the Earth now, we will spoil it for the people of the future.

Can I help care for the Earth?

There are many things you can do in your everyday life to care for the Earth. This book tells you about some of them. Just think, if everyone did the same as you, Earth would be a better place to live.

Our Solar System has nine planets which orbit the Sun.

Is it true?
There is no other planet like Earth.

Yes. There is only one Earth. It is special – it is the only planet known to have life on it. Perhaps one day life will be found on another planet, too.

Amazing!
There has been life on Earth for approximately 3.5 billion years.

Is Earth's climate changing?
Earth's climate is slowly getting warmer. Scientists who study the climate have found that it is a little warmer now than it was 100 years ago. You may not notice the difference, but plants and animals do.

Climate study in the Antarctic

Is it true?
Trees reduce carbon dioxide in the atmosphere.

Yes. Tree leaves take harmful carbon dioxide from the atmosphere and give out oxygen. We breathe the oxygen they make.

Why is the temperature rising?

It's getting warmer because of what the Earth's 6 billion people are doing. Because of the way we lead our lives, we are changing the Earth's climate. We are making the planet grow warmer.

Amazing! There is far more carbon dioxide in the atmosphere than there was 200 years ago. This is mainly why it's warmer today than it was in the past.

How are we making the temperature rise?

By burning 'fossil fuels' – coal, oil and natural gas – we are putting 'greenhouse gases', such as carbon dioxide, into the atmosphere. The gases surround the Earth and keep heat in.

Cars and factories burn 'fossil fuels' which produce harmful 'greenhouse gases'.

What will happen as the temperature rises?

As the Earth's climate warms up, glaciers and the ice at the North and South Poles will melt, causing the sea level to rise. This will bring floods, and some islands will disappear. Deserts will spread, and droughts will occur.

Amazing! Cows are making the temperature rise. The smelly greenhouse gas methane comes from animals, such as cows, and from factories. Humans make it, too!

How can governments reduce carbon dioxide levels?

Burning gasoline in cars puts carbon dioxide into the atmosphere. Governments can build transport systems that don't make carbon dioxide, and order more trees to be planted.

Electric railway

 What can I do to help?
Use less electricity. This is because most electricity comes from burning fossil fuels which makes carbon dioxide. Switch off lights, TVs and computers when not in use.

Is it true?
If the Antarctic ice sheet melted, the sea level would rise.

Yes. It holds two-thirds of the Earth's fresh water. If it melted, the sea would rise by up to 230 feet. Coastlines would change all over the world.

Antarctica

What other problems are caused by burning fossil fuels?

Sulfur dioxide is another harmful gas that comes from power stations and vehicles. It is very acidic, which means it eats things away. In the atmosphere, it mixes with droplets of moisture to make acid rain. Trees die when acid rain falls on them and on their soil.

Is it true?
Some polystyrene burger cartons are bad for the Earth's atmosphere.

Yes. Some of them are because they're made using chemicals that damage the ozone layer. Many cartons are now made without these harmful chemicals.

Is Earth's atmosphere being harmed?

There is a layer of helpful gas around the Earth called ozone. It protects us from the Sun's dangerous ultraviolet rays. Unfortunately, the ozone layer is damaged because humans have put harmful chemicals into the atmosphere.

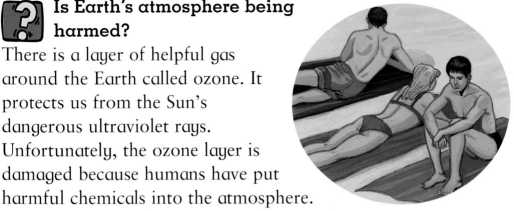

WARNING! Always use a sunscreen in sunny weather to protect your skin from the Sun's rays.

Scandinavian forest damaged by acid rain

 Amazing! When a nuclear power station at Chernobyl, Ukraine, exploded in 1986, radioactive material was sent into the atmosphere. Animals across Europe were contaminated by the radiation.

Underground storage of nuclear waste

Is nuclear power dangerous?

Nuclear power stations do not burn fossil fuels. Therefore, they do not make harmful gases. But they do make radioactive waste material. It is dangerous and will have to be guarded for many years into the future.

491

 Are animals in danger?
Thousands of different
animals live on Earth. It is their
planet, as well as ours. Sadly,
because of what we do, many
animals are in danger. An oil
spill at sea harms seals, birds and
fish. When forests are cut down,
many animals lose their homes.

Oil spill

 **How many kinds of animals
are in danger?**
There are many thousands of
different kinds of animals in danger.
Some are so rare they are endangered.
This means they are almost extinct –
they have almost died out. If that
happens, they will have gone forever.

Endangered species

What is being done to save animals?

Many endangered animals are now protected by law. It is wrong for people to harm them, or the places where they live. Some endangered animals are bred in zoos. This helps to increase their numbers.

Golden lion tamarin

Amazing! Passenger pigeons used to form flocks of millions of birds, but they were hunted to extinction in the wild. The very last one, named Martha, died in 1914.

Cormorant covered in oil

Is it true? Humans are causing animals to die out.

Yes. It's said that one kind of animal dies out every 30 minutes because of what we're doing to the planet.

Rainforest

Why are forests good for the Earth?

Forests are the 'lungs' of the planet. Their trees make much of the oxygen we breathe. Forests provide us with food and timber. Some medicines are made from plants found only in forests.

Are forests in danger?

Forests are in danger in many parts of the world. In some countries trees are killed by acid rain. Elsewhere, whole forests are cut down for their timber, or to make way for farm land.

Logger truck

What is being done to save forests?

Some governments have stopped cutting down the forests on their land. Many forests that are left are protected by law. Also, new forests are being planted, to grow timber like any other crop. It is grown to be cut down.

 Amazing! Since 1980, an area of tropical forest six times the size of France has been turned into farm land, or plantations of oil palm, rubber and other crops.

 Is it true?
Soil erosion can be seen from space.

Yes. Trees keep soil in place. Where forests are cleared the soil wears away, or erodes, until only rock is left.

Soil erosion on Madagascar, seen from space

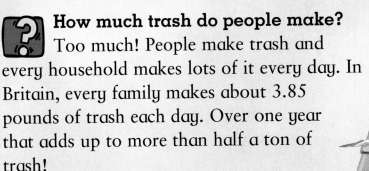

How much trash do people make?

Too much! People make trash and every household makes lots of it every day. In Britain, every family makes about 3.85 pounds of trash each day. Over one year that adds up to more than half a ton of trash!

Is it true?
Some trash is dumped at sea.

Trash dump

Yes. Every day thousands of tons of trash are thrown into the sea. The seabed is littered with trash, such as bits of plastic, that never rot away.

Trash dumped at sea

What happens to all this trash?

Because so much trash is made, it's a problem to deal with it all. Some is burned inside furnaces. A lot is buried on the land. Some trash is collected and sent for recycling.

Burning trash in a furnace

Amazing! The world's trash mountain grows by about 2 million tons every day.

What can I do to make less trash?

Put the three R's into practice: Reduce, Reuse, Recycle. Reduce means use less of something. Reuse means use something again. Recycle is to save something so it can be made into a new thing.

? What can I do with kitchen and garden waste?

Vegetable peelings, tea leaves and grass cuttings are 'green' waste. If you pile them into a heap in the garden, they will rot down to make compost.

Even some kinds of paper can be turned into compost.

? Why is compost good for the environment?

Compost is food for the soil. It contains nutrients (foods) which keep soil healthy. Using home-made compost means less peat compost is dug up from natural places, and animals' homes are saved.

Gardening with compost

Are there other ways of recycling green waste?

You don't need a garden to recycle green waste! You can make small amounts of compost and plant food inside a wormery – a container where a colony of worms live. Worm bins can be kept inside or outside.

Is it true?
Leaves make good compost.

Yes. Leaves rot down slowly to become leaf mold. Put them in a black bag or an open-topped wire cage. After two years you'll have compost.

Amazing! Green waste in a rubbish tip makes dangerous methane gas, and liquid that can pollute water and kill wildlife. It's safer to make it into compost.

Polluted river

What can I do at home?

Inside the house, start your own recycling center, collecting materials that can be recycled. Reuse plastic bags, switch off electrical items when they're not in use, and don't leave faucets dripping. Outside, get composting, and grow your own organic vegetables.

Amazing!
Even an alien would think Earth needs caring for. That's because there are 100,000 pieces of space junk whizzing around the planet.

Energy-efficient house

Insulation to keep the heat in

Switch off electrical items after use

Don't leave faucets dripping

Cycling is energy-efficient and good exercise.

Grow your own organic vegetables.

What can I do at school?

If your school has a Green Club, join it. If it doesn't, ask if one can be started. As at home, switch off lights when they're not in use, and collect paper, cans and glass for recycling. Walk or cycle to school. Try to use cars less.

Is it true? You can make a difference.

Yes. Imagine if everyone in your class, your street, even your town recycled things. What a difference that would make!

Sorting trash for recycling

How can I find out more?

If you would like to help make the Earth a better, safer place to live, now and in the future, you might like to join groups such as Greenpeace, Friends of the Earth or World Wide Fund for Nature. Your library will have their addresses.

Sort your trash for recycling.

GLOSSARY

Abdomen The back part of an insect or arachnid's body.

Acid rain Rain that contains chemicals that are harmful to nature.

Active A volcano that is still erupting.

Aerofoil A sail or wing with a curved surface to give lift off the water or ground.

Air bladder An air-filled sac that helps keep fish afloat. Sharks do not have an air bladder, but have a huge oily liver instead.

Air brake A network of brakes along a train that uses compressed air to squeeze the brakes closed.

Airship A lighter-than-air aircraft with engines to make it move along.

Algae Tiny plants that live in water.

Amber Once liquid tree resin (sap) that has been fossilized.

Amphibian An animal that lives on land and in water, such as a frog.

Amphibious Capable of moving both on land and in the water.

Antennae A pair of 'feelers' on the head, which help an animal taste, smell and touch.

Anti-freeze A chemical which prevents water, blood and other liquids from freezing solid.

Ape A tailless primate; a gorilla, orang-utan, chimp, bonobo, gibbon or siamang.

Arachnid Member of the group of animals that includes spiders, scorpions and mites.

Articulated A vehicle that is capable of bending in the middle.

Asteroid A small rocky body which orbits the Sun.

Astrology Using patterns in the sky as a guide to daily life.

Astronaut Someone who travels into space. The word means 'sailor of the stars'.

Astronomer A scientist who studies space, normally using telescopes.

Astronomy The science of space-watching.

Atmosphere The gases or air surrounding a planet.

Axis The imaginary line around which a planet spins.

Axle A straight rod at the base of a vehicle, which connects a pair of wheels.

Bacteria Tiny, living things that live in soil, water and the air.

Balaclava A hat which covers all of the head and neck, with just a hole for the face.

Baleen Long, tough bristles hanging down inside some whales' mouths. They are used for sieving food from the sea. Only great whales, such as the blue whale have baleen.

Bark The tough protective outer layer of a tree, which covers and protects the trunk and the roots.

Barnacles Tiny shellfish that grow on rocks and the bottom of ships. Barnacles also stick to whales' backs.

Bear Family of carnivores including brown bears, polar bears and grizzly bears.

Big Bang The huge explosion that created the Universe around 15 billion years ago.

Biplane A small plane with two pairs of wings.

Black hole A place in space with such strong gravity that not even light can escape from it.

Blizzard A winter storm with strong winds and heavy snow.

Blowhole The hole on top of a whale's head that it uses for breathing out.

Blubber A thick layer of fat under a sea mammal's skin, which protects it from the cold.

Body shell A strong metal shell that is the main part of a modern car.

Boosters The parts of a rocket used to push a spacecraft into orbit.

Bow The front part of a ship. It is normally pointed to break easily through the water.

Brakes Devices that slow a vehicle. They work by pressing pads firmly against the spinning wheels.

Butte A small, flat-topped hill in the desert.

Camouflage A special coloring or pattern on the surface of an animal, which makes it blend in with its background, making it difficult to see, and less

likely to be attacked by another animal.

Canines The pointy teeth in a carnivore's jaw, used for tearing into flesh.

Capsule A small spacecraft with room for one or two crew.

Carnivore Any mammal, or other animal, that eats only meat and that has teeth adapted for eating meat.

Carrion The dead body of an animal.

Cartilage A rubbery, flexible material. The skeletons of sharks, rays and skate are made of cartilage.

Cat Family of carnivores divided into big cats that roar (lions, tigers, jaguars and leopards) and small cats that purr.

Chassis The central base of a vehicle, on to which the axles and bodywork are attached.

Climate The weather conditions in a particular place on Earth.

Clutch A device on a vehicle, which controls whether or not the power from an engine reaches the wheels.

Cold-blooded Animals that cannot control their own body temperature. Instead,

they have to rely on the weather to warm them up or cool them down.

Colony A large group of animals living together. Honeybees, ants, termites and some birds all live in colonies.

Comet A ball of rock and ice which passes through the solar system, emitting long glowing tails, as it nears the sun.

Coniferous Trees that have needle-like leaves and cones, such as cedar, fir and spruce trees.

Constellation The pattern that stars seem to make in the sky, from our viewpoint on Earth.

Container A metal box on a ship, truck or train that can be filled with cargo.

Convertible A car with a fabric roof which folds down for open-air driving.

Core The middle of something.

Cosmology The science of how the Universe (or 'cosmos') works.

Cosmonaut A Russian or Soviet astronaut. The word means 'sailor of the Universe'.

Cretaceous period The third period in dinosaur

history, which lasted from 135 million years ago until the extinction of the dinosaurs about 65 million years ago.

Crust The solid layer of rock on the surface of the Earth. It is about 5 miles thick under the sea, and 25 miles thick under the continents.

Cumulonimbus Another name for a tall, dark thundercloud.

Cylinder A chamber inside an engine inside which pistons move up and down.

Cynodont A type of reptile with fur, which evolved into mammals.

Dam A barrier built across a river to stop it flooding or to collect water in a reservoir.

Delta The end of a river where it flows into the sea.

Dinosaur A type of reptile that once lived on Earth, but which has died out.

Dormant A sleeping volcano that could erupt at any time.

Drought A time of very dry weather when less rain than normal falls.

Denticle The sharp points on a shark's skin.

Dog Family of carnivores including wolves, foxes and jackals.

Diesel engine A type of internal combustion engine that uses diesel oil as fuel.

Drag A force caused by air flowing around a moving object that slows it down.

Drive shaft A rod that links an engine with the wheels of a vehicle. The engine turns the rod, which turns the wheels.

Dug-out A type of canoe made by hollowing out a large tree trunk.

Echo-location The way that some animals use sound to locate food and find their way around. They make sounds that hit solid objects and send back echoes. From these, the animals can tell what the objects are, and where they are.

Eclipse When light from the Sun or Moon is blocked out. A solar eclipse is when the Moon passes between the Earth and Sun, casting a shadow on the Earth. A lunar eclipse is when Earth passes between the Moon and Sun.

Embryo A stage in development after an egg is fertilized until the young animal is born or hatches.

Endangered At risk of dying out.

Evolution A gradual change in form over many generations.

Engineer A person who uses scientific knowledge to make useful things such as trains or bridges.

Equator The imaginary line that runs around the middle of the Earth.

Exhaust pipes Metal pipes which direct the waste gases from the engine into the air.

Extinct No longer alive anywhere on Earth or a volcano that has stopped erupting.

Falconer Someone who breeds and trains falcons and hawks.

Fangs Special teeth through which snakes squirt poison into their enemies or prey.

Fault A crack in the Earth's crust.

Flock A large group of birds.

Flying boat A plane with a fuselage shaped like a boat's hull, which can take off and land on water.

Fold mountain A mountain made when one piece of the Earth's crust crashed into another and pushes up the land in between.

Fossil The remains of an ancient animal or plant preserved in rock.

Fossil fuels Fuels such as coal, oil and gas, made from fossilized remains.

Freshwater Water that does not taste salty. Rivers and many lakes are freshwater.

Fuselage The main part of a plane where passengers and crew sit and cargo is carried.

Galaxy A family of star systems that are held together by gravity. Our Solar System is in the Milky Way galaxy.

Gas engine An engine in which the pistons are pushed out by a mixture of gas and air exploding.

Gears Sets of cogs which transfer power from a vehicle's engine to its wheels. By selecting different gears, the driver can start off and travel at different speeds.

Generator A machine which converts movement into electricity.

Genes Special instructions inside every cell of a living being, which tell it how to grow.

Gills Breathing slits behind the head of a fish, used to extract oxygen from water.

Gizzard A special second stomach that birds have, with strong muscles to help grind up and digest food.

Glider A plane without an engine.

Gravity The force of attraction between objects, such as you and the Earth.

Greenhouse gas Gases, such as carbon dioxide or methane, which surround the Earth and keep heat in.

Grooming Cleaning the fur of ticks and fleas. Primates often do this for each other.

Ground Control A big team of experts on Earth who look after each space mission.

Habitat The type of place where an animal or plant lives in the wild. The polar bear's habitat is the icy Arctic.

Heatshield A special skin for spacecraft, to prevent burning up on the return to Earth.

Helper monkey A monkey that has been bred and trained to help and live with a disabled owner.

Herbivore An animal that eats only plants.

Hibernation A deep sleep-like state which many warm and cold-blooded animals go into to survive through the winter.

Horseless carriage Early cars, which looked like horse-drawn carriages, but had engines instead of horses.

Horsepower A measurement of engine power equal to 745.7 watts. A family car produces around 150 horsepower per tonne.

Hull The main part of ship or boat. It keeps the boat watertight and supports the decks.

Hydraulic Worked by liquid. Liquid pumped to the cylinders moves pistons in or out to make a machine's parts move.

Hydroplane A light, flat-bottomed motorboat, which skims along the surface of the water, when driven at high speed.

Ichthyosaurs Marine reptiles that were alive in dinosaur times.

Indicators Flashing lights which tell other drivers which way a car is about to turn.

Insect Small animal with three body parts – the head, thorax and abdomen, and three pairs of legs.

Internal combustion engine A machine that converts the energy in fuel into movement by burning it with air inside cylinders.

Jet engine An engine that pushes an aircraft forwards by burning liquid fuel, and sending a jet of hot gas backwards.

Junction A point where two or more railway tracks are joined.

Jurassic period The second period in dinosaur history, which lasted from 200 - 135 million years ago.

Knot The measurement of speed at sea. One knot equals 1.16 mph.

Krill Tiny, shrimp-like sea creatures. Huge amounts of krill are eaten by whales

Larva The young stage of a hatched insect, which looks different from the adult.

Lava What magma is called when it erupts from a volcano.

Laser An intense beam of light that can be used to transfer energy across space.

Lens A curved piece of glass.

Lethal Deadly, or fatal.

Light Year The distance light travels in a year, roughly 6 million million miles.

Lightning conductor A rod on the roof of a tall building that is attached to a strip of metal. It carries electricity from the lightning safely down to the ground.

Liquid Oxygen Oxygen is the gas in the air that allows things to burn. Rockets carry oxygen in liquid form to burn where there is no air.

Litter Baby animals born from the same mother at the same time.

Lobtailing When whales slap their tails on the surface of the sea, as a signal to other whales.

Mach The measurement of the speed of sound – Mach 2 is twice the speed of sound.

Magma Rock deep beneath the Earth. It is so hot that it has melted.

Magnets Objects that attract or repel metal. In trains, very strong magnets are powered by electricity.

Mammal A warm-blooded animal covered in fur that gives birth to live young and feeds its babies on mother's milk.

Mantle The part of the Earth between its crust and its central core.

Maori The name for the native people of New Zealand and their language.

Marsupial A mammal that gives birth to very undeveloped live young, that live at first in their mother's pouch.

Meander A large bend in a river. Sometimes a meander gets cut off and forms an oxbow lake.

Mesa A large, flat-topped hill in the desert.

Meteorite A rock that flies through outer space until it lands on Earth, sometimes with disastrous results.

Meteoroid A small lump of space rock.

Migrate To move from one place to another, often far away. Birds and animals may migrate to find warmer places to live each winter.

Mimicry When an animal or bird copies another. Some parrots and mynah birds can even mimic the sound of the telephone.

Missile A weapon that is thrown through the air.

Module A section of a space station.

Monkey Usually a primate with a tail, although not all monkeys have tails.

Monoplane A plane with one pair of wings.

Moon Any large, roughly ball-shaped natural satellite orbiting a planet.

Navigator The person in an aircraft who plans the aircraft's route and works out where the aircraft is.

Nebula A huge cloud of gas and dust where new stars are born.

Nectar Sugary liquid produced by plants, and collected by insects. Honeybees use nectar to make honey.

Nuclear power Power made from radioactive material.

Nuclear waste Dangerous waste material from nuclear power plants.

Nutrients Chemicals dissolved in water, used by plants in order to grow.

Observatory A place that houses telescopes and other instruments for viewing the sky.

Omnivore An animal that eats both meat and plants.

Orbit To travel around.

Organic A living thing, or something made from a living thing.

Oxygen A gas that animals breathe in and which keeps them alive.

Paddle wheel A wheel with flat blades around the out-side. The bottom of the wheel sits in the water. As a ship's paddle wheel turns, the paddles push the ship along.

Paleontologist A person who studies fossilized remains.

Paralyze To make an animal helpless so that it cannot move.

Parasite A tiny animal that lives in or on another animal from which it gets its food. Parasites are often harmful to their 'host'.

Payload The cargo that a rocket carries into space.

Peat A dark brown material made from rotten plants.

Pedigree A domestic (not wild) animal that has been bred to have certain characteristics.

Pistons Sliding parts inside an engine that push the wheels around.

Planet A body of gas or rock orbiting a star, usually more than 620 miles wide. Planets are not massive enough to be stars. They shine because they reflect the light of the star they are orbiting.

Plankton Tiny animals and plants that float in the sea. Some of the larger sharks and several types of whales feed only on plankton that they filter from the water.

Platform The area in a railway station, where passengers get in and out of trains.

Plesiosaurs Marine reptiles with large flippers, which were alive in dinosaur times.

Pneumatic Worked by air pressure, or containing air.

Pods The name for family groups of dolphins, seals and whales.

Poles The points at either end of a planet's axis, known as the north and south poles.

Pollution The mess caused by fuel-burning machines, which can be dangerous.

Predator An animal that hunts other animals for food.

Preening When a bird combs and tidies its feathers with its beak.

Prehistoric An ancient time before writing was invented.

Prey An animal that is hunted by another animal for food.

Pride A group of lions that live together.

Primate A group of big-brained mammals, with forward facing eyes, made up of six different groups: lemurs; lorises and galagos; tarsiers; New World monkeys; Old World monkeys; and apes and humans.

Propeller A set of blades. When a ship's propeller spins round in the water, it pushes the ship along.

Pterosaurs Reptiles that traveled through the air in prehistoric times.

Pulsar A small, dense, fast-spinning neutron star that gives out regular pulses of light and radio waves.

Pupa A larva enters the pupa stage before turning into an adult insect. A butterfly pupa is called a chrysalis.

Quasar A region of space giving off more energy than almost any other.

Radiation Dangerous rays, for example those from the Sun. On Earth, the atmosphere blocks most of the Sun's radiation, but in space special shields are needed.

Radiator Part of the cooling system of a car. Air flowing past the radiator cools the hot water that has taken heat from the engine.

Radioactive A substance that gives off harmful rays and particles.

Rainforest An evergreen tropical forest where there is heavy rainfall most days.

Radar A machine which sends radio waves into the sky and works out where objects are by detecting how the waves bounce back.

Rechargeable Describes a battery that can have its electricity replaced after it has run down. All cars have a rechargeable battery.

Reservoirs Lakes used for storing water.

Roll-cage A strong metal frame that surrounds the driver of a roofless racing car. If a car flips upside down, the roll-cage makes the car roll over into an upright position.

Rudder A flap at the stern of a ship or boat that turns from side to side to make the ship or boat turn left or right.

Saltwater crocodile Also known as the Estuarine crocodile, they are the largest crocodiles, and can also live in fresh water.

Sauropods Large plant-eating dinosaurs that included Diplodocus.

School A large number of the same kind of fish all swimming together. Hammerhead sharks swim in schools.

Seaplane A plane with floats instead of wheels for its undercarriage, for landing on water.

Seasons Different times of the year, when Earth's weather and life change according to the position of the Sun in the sky.

Sidecar A single-wheeled car with a seat that attaches to the side of a motorbicycle.

Soil erosion Wearing away of the soil.

Solar panels Mirrors that capture energy from the Sun and turn it into electricity.

Solar power Power made from the Sun.

Solar System Our Sun and everything that travels around it.

Space station A huge satellite with living space for a crew of astronauts and scientists.

Stabilizers Small extra wheels on each side of a bicycle or motorbicycle that stop it toppling over sideways.

Stage A section of a rocket. Rockets usually have three stages.

Stalactite A spike made of stone that grows downwards from the ceiling of a cave.

Stalagmite A spike made of stone that grows upwards from the floor of a cave.

Star A huge ball of super-hot burning gas.

Steam engine A type of engine in which the pistons are moved inside cylinders by the pressure of steam created in a boiler.

Stern The back part of a ship.

Submersible An underwater vehicle like a small submarine.

Supercharger A mechanical pump which increases the amount of air taken into an engine to make it more powerful.

Suspension The series of springs and dampers on the underside of a vehicle. The suspension allows the vehicle to travel comfortably over bumps on the road.

Talons Long, curved claws. Birds of prey use their talons to grip and tear at their prey.

Tarn A small mountain lake carved out by ice millions of years ago.

Telescope An instrument that makes distant objects seem bigger and nearer. They collect light, radio waves, X-rays or other waves.

Tendon A strong cord which connects a muscle to a bone.

Territory The patch of land or sea in which an animal lives. Many animals fiercely defend their territory.

Throttle The device on a car or motorbicycle, also known as the accelerator, which controls the flow of fuel to the engine.

Torpedo An underwater missile that explodes when it hits a ship.

Tractor unit The front section of an articulated truck, where the cab and engine are located.

Trailer The rear section of an articulated truck, where the cargo is carried.

Trams Electric trains which run in city streets, cleaner and quieter than buses.

Tread The pattern of grooves around the outside of a tire.

Triassic period The first period in dinosaur history, which lasted from 225 - 200 million years ago, when the first of the dinosaurs appeared on Earth.

Tar A black, sticky, waterproof substance that goes runny when it is heated up and hardens again when it cools.

Tricycle A bicycle or motorbicycle with three wheels, normally one at the front and two at the rear.

Triplane A plane with three sets of wings.

Twister Another name for a tornado.

Ultraviolet rays Harmful rays from the Sun.

Undercarriage The lower section of a plane. The undercarriage of most planes is the wheels, but seaplanes have floats, and ski planes land using skis.

Universe Everything that exists.

Vacuum An empty space with no air.

Venom Poison.

Vertebrates Animals that have a spine inside their bodies. Vertebrates include mammals, birds, reptiles and amphibians

Wormhole A short cut between two different parts of space.

INDEX